Decision Made

(No Turning Back)

James Perry

This book is dedicated to my four children from whom I have
learned much over the years…
Elizabeth Lee Perry Barron
James Andrew Perry
Martha Ruth Perry Davis
Rebecca Lois Perry Buice Taggart

And Also
Dedicated to their Mother, my precious wife, who lovingly
nurtured them and patiently taught them…
Peggy Ann Fry Perry

Foreword

Many years ago my Dad asked me to read over his books to catch any errors – spelling, punctuation, etc. – before he sent them to publication. In the midst of proof reading this book, Dad asked me to write a forward. What? I am the person who bleeds red ink, sends inquiring questions and highlights passages in various colors that cause consternation when I return the chapters to him – I am the person in the shadows. And yet, I am the one who has read every single book he has written and have a window into the heart and soul of James Perry.

Dad has a passion for his Lord and Savior and a desire in his heart to share that passion to all who will listen. My first memory of Dad's passion for God was when I was a little girl and we lived in Seaside Heights, NJ. We would roll tracts in colorful cellophane paper so they looked like candy sticks. Then on the weekends during the summer he would take the tracts, go to the boardwalk with other men from the church, hand out the tracts and minister to anyone who would listen. Reflecting back, I'm sure he faced much derision from those who were out to party and participate in all the boardwalk had to offer. And yet he faithfully made the decision to follow God's call to spread the gospel in all places, at all times no matter the cost, which brings us to Dad's current book, *Decision Made*.

Within the pages of this book you will be challenged to examine the decision made to follow God's call to live a life in accordance with His will. Through a study of the lives of Joshua and Caleb we will see what a serious God expects of those he calls – will we be bold and courageous and stand firmly in God's will as did Moses, Joshua and Caleb or will we whine and complain and long for a life that seems easier but leaves us enslaved and on a path that leads to death as did a generation of Israelites. Will we pick up the mantle and teach the next generation the ways of God – His laws and their application to our lives. Will we be a "small boat" like Rahab who performed a small act which led to an unknown reward that reverberated throughout generations.

In today's world many decisions made are contrary to God's will. This last weekend we witnessed mass shootings in El Paso, Texas and Dayton, Ohio. Thousands of our children are sacrificed on the altar of abortion each year. Marriage, instituted by God between a man and a woman, has transformed into "marry whomever you love". We can't even define a family or who is a man or woman. The following passage that I reviewed in the book several nights ago has stuck in my mind: "Deuteronomy 31:16-18 contains the Lord's concern about the potential behavior of the generation entering The Promised Land. 'The Lord said to Moses: Behold, you are about to lie down with your fathers. Then this people will rise and whore after the foreign gods among them in the land that they are entering, and they will forsake me and break my covenant that I have made with them. Then my anger will be kindled against them in that day, and I will forsake them and hide my face from them, and they will be devoured. And many evils and troubles will come upon them, so that they will say in that day, Have not these evils come upon us because our God is not among us? And I will surely hide my face in that day because of all the evil that they have done, because they have turned to other gods.' The Lord is indicating that temptations within the new horizon culture will have an influence on many of the people and those influences will infiltrate their belief system….They have a choice of daring to be different and live as the Lord's people or willingly adapt their lives and lifestyle to the culture that exists."

"A guideline and requirement for older men is given in Titus 2:2, 'Older men are to be sober-minded, dignified, self-controlled, sound in faith, in love, and in steadfastness.' In other words, they are to be examples for the next generation to whom the torch of faith is to be passed." And this is exactly how you should see my dad and then read the words of wisdom within these pages. Like Joshua and Caleb, he made the decision to see all the good of God's promises and know that God will make all things possible in His time to those who follow His lead no matter the obstacles of the culture. Dad is in his 85th year of life, 56 of those years have been spent in service to God. He made the decision to follow God no matter the cost – he is calling you to do the same. Read and be challenged to discover the great value in the decision made to follow God.

Beth Barron
Schertz, Texas

Table of Contents

Introduction.. 1

1. Getting Started 5

2. Fail-Safe.. 9

3. Good Courage 13

4. Unmixed 17

5. Adjustments 21

6. Severity.. 25

7. Discipline... 29

8. Complicity 33

9. Tough Love... 37

10. Adaptation... 41

11. Patience.. 45

12. Distractions 49

13. Energized 53

14. Darkness 57

15. Unheralded.. 61

16. Expectation 65

17. Misdirection... 69

18. Meditating... 73

19. Compliance 77

20. The Master's Plan.. 81

21. First Steps 85

22. New Horizons 89

23. A Journey Ends 93

24. Unfolding Plan 97

25. Spies Sent Out 101

26. A Covenant Promise 105

27. Stepping Out 109

28. New Environments 113

29. Eagerness 117

30. Overcoming Obstacles 121

31. Faith Faltering 125

32. Battle Strategy 129

33. Staying Strong 133

34. Definitive Choice 137

Epilogue 141

Introduction

One's life involves many choices, decisions and commitments. Where one will live; what occupation one will seek; the best education for the occupation choice; a life partner; etc. Historically, our nation had preferred to be more isolationist than involved in the various nations of the world. As George Washington approached the climax of his second term as President, he penned a Farewell Address. As he focused upon the unity of the nation, he also clearly intended that the nation should avoid entangling alliances. This more or less was held dearly by the nation. It was with the greatest reluctance that compromise was made with that avowed commitment of the nation.

This was obvious at the start of War in Europe in the late 1930s. Winston Churchill was relentless in his appeal to the President of the United States, Franklin D. Roosevelt, to come to the aid of Great Britain that was under siege by the constant attacks of Germany. Reluctantly, agreement was reached to send equipment and supplies. In sailing across the Atlantic Ocean, the German Submarine fleet torpedoed and sank many Merchant Ships and the supplies so desperately needed by England sank to the floor of the Ocean.

After Japan attacked Pearl Harbor in December 1941, the view of being isolationist came to a halt as the United States set out to defend itself. Shortly thereafter, it was obvious the world was at war and the United States aligned itself with Great Britain in their defense. The battles in the Atlantic and Pacific Oceans would take a heavy toll of lives, ships that were sunk and collateral damage resulting from the constant bombing by Germany and the Kamikaze attacks by Japan.

The Cover is a snapshot of the D-Day Invasion – June 6, 1944. After careful consideration of the English Channel Tides and the weather factors, a decision was made to proceed across the Channel and encounter the occupying forces of Germany in France. General Dwight D. Eisenhower addressed the troops before they set out on their mission:

> Soldiers, Sailors, and Airmen of the Allied Expeditionary Force: You are about to embark upon the Great Crusade, toward which we have striven these many months. The eyes of the world are upon you. The hopes and prayers of liberty-loving people everywhere march with you...Your task will not be an easy one. Your enemy is well trained, well equipped, and battle-hardened. He will fight savagely...I have full confidence in your courage, devotion to duty, and skill in battle. We will accept nothing less than full victory...Let us all beseech the blessing of Almighty God on this great and noble undertaking." (Dwight D. Eisenhower)

An irony to this war is that most of the Generals had never fired a gun in combat. Yet, the lives of hundreds and thousands of loyal soldiers were inspired to fight the fight to set a world free from tyrants and dictators.

In the spiritual encounters and noble undertakings, the Biblical Christian is called upon to pursue, Jesus reminded and cautioned them: "No one who puts his hand to the plow and looks back is fit for the kingdom of God." The truth being conveyed is that once one has decided to follow Jesus, there is no longer the option for one to turn back. Hebrews 11 is a listing of those who accomplished exploits for the Lord. It is not an exhaustive list. This is indicated by the summary words in verses 33-34 of the many others "who through faith conquered kingdoms, enforced justice, obtained promises, stopped the mouths of lions, quenched the power of fire, escaped the edge of the sword, were made strong out of weakness, became mighty in war, put foreign armies to flight." One whose name is unlisted is Caleb. He, along with Joshua, were the key men with Moses as he set out on the journey to the promised land. It was said these men, and repeatedly about Caleb (Numbers 32:12): "Caleb son of Jephunneh the Kenizzite and Joshua son of Nun - they followed the LORD wholeheartedly. To do anything wholeheartedly requires total sincerity, genuine enthusiasm and focused commitment to a cause or person. Very often, one will be in the minority. This is what occurred when the 12 men were chosen by Moses to assess the Canaan – the land of promise. When they returned with their report (Numbers 13-14), there was basic agreement among the twelve – the land was beautiful and the produce of it was luxurious.

One word is introduced that changes the entire report from being one that is positive to one that is overwhelming negative. The word is – "however" – (Numbers 13:28). Whenever this word is introduced into one's opportunity and possibility, the focus will shift from being positive to being negative; from being possible to being impossible.

The majority (10 spies) introduce the challenge of having to confront strong people; fortified cities; very tall and strong men; plus those who have lived there all of their lives. The conclusion of the majority – don't go! We aren't equal to the enormity of the task (Numbers 13:28-29).

Numbers 14 indicates the people willingly embraced the description of the majority and begin to murmur and complain about Moses and his leadership. They even allow that gloom, despair and death is all that is on their immediate horizon. They begin to circulate that they were better off in Egypt and should return to the place from which they had been delivered. In verse 6 through 10, Joshua and Caleb address the murmuring people. They appeal to the people that the protection of the inhabitants of Canaan has been removed. They emphasize that The Lord is with us and will prevail in the conquest of the land. They state boldly that there is no

3

need to fear the people of the land when the Lord is on your side. They underscore – that while there will be several challenges and difficulties – with the Lord on our side, we are well able to possess and conquer the land. When the murmuring is reaching its peak – suddenly – the glory of the Lord appeared at the tent of meeting to all the people of Israel. The people will need to stay focused on the Lord and His glory. They need to be committed to the one who has called them and who will never leave them or forsake them.

There continues to be the needed commitment and focus among the people of God today – those who will courageously follow the Lord wholeheartedly. That which caused their associates to falter when faced with great challenges was the absence of a focus upon a great God Who is able to do immeasurably more that anyone can ask, think or imagine. There was a great challenge and opportunity before them but they erred by yielding to their strength to overcome rather than to God's power that is more than sufficient through the great power that is available to God's people and that is in those who believe and follow Him.

Luke 8:14 indicates the people's absence of focus. It is described by the Word of God that was distributed to them but they allowed it to fall "among the thorns. They are those who hear, but as they go on their way they are choked and suffocated by the cares, riches and pleasures of life, and the seeds are unable to bear fruit and mature."

The Message paraphrase indicates the life-style choice: "The seed is crowded out and nothing comes of it as the people go about with their lives. They will experience worrying about tomorrow, making money and having fun." There needs to be a removal of the thorns and weeds that have choked and suffocated the Word in the lives of the people. They will need to commit themselves to following the Lord wholeheartedly.

1. Getting Started

Decisions – if based upon foundational principles and core values - are relatively easy to make. It's when the unexpected occurs or confusing data is being considered that decisions and choices become more difficult. The greatest influences in the family where I was reared had some foundational principles that were not to be compromised. My Grandmother, Isabella MacLain Smith, had legally immigrated to this country in the early 1900s. She had some pithy statements (principles) that she would use with my brother, my sister and me. One of them, especially when we were going out somewhere on our own, was her reminder: "Remember – Thou God seest me." Our Mother had a phrase she would often use verbally or in correspondence, "A good start usually assures a good finish."

This book is not intended to be a biography about Caleb although reference will be made about him. The primary statement that summarizes his life is that: "Caleb wholeheartedly (faithfully) followed the Lord." We learn a valuable lesson about him when the decision about proceeding to Canaan – The Promised Land – became an issue. Caleb and Joshua were two of the twelve spies who travelled throughout Canaan to bring back a report that would serve to generate enthusiasm and rejoicing by the children of Israel as they proceeded to their new home country. That plan was thwarted when ten of the twelve spies raised some misgivings and negatives that would await the Israelites if they proceeded.

The ten negative spies had a great influence upon the people (Numbers 14). Their report caused an uproar among the people and a great emotional reaction that lasted throughout the night. The people approached Moses and Aaron with murmuring, grumbling and complaint. The people were united in their outcry and stated their two conclusions:

(1) It would be better for them to return to Egypt (despite the oppression and slavery from which the Lord was delivering them); and (2) They unitedly agreed they needed to choose a new leader who knew the way back to Egypt.

Moses and Aaron did not respond with anger or accusation toward these misguided souls. Along with Joshua and Caleb they fell on their faces before the people and pleaded with them to reconsider their expressed desire to go back. The decision had been made by the Lord that they were to inherit the land and there was no option for them to turn back. Joshua and Caleb emphasized that the Lord brought them toward this exceedingly good land and He could be depended upon to bring everyone safely into His land of promise for His people. The Lord was annoyed with the behavior and decision of the people. In His disgust, the Lord said to Moses: "How long will this people despise Me? How long will they not believe in Me? I will strike them with the pestilence and disinherit them" (Numbers 14:11-12).

Moses intervened for the people by reminding the Lord that the people inhabiting all the other nations would think that He was unable to control and protect His own people. Moses' plea is one of compassion as he states to the Lord (Numbers 14:19), "Please pardon the iniquity of this people, according to the greatness of your steadfast love, just as you have forgiven this people, from Egypt until now." The Lord responded affirmatively with the stipulation that no one who was opposed to going forward would ever be permitted to enter the Promised Land. They would wander in the wilderness until they all had died. However, "Your little ones, who you said would become a prey, I will bring in, and they shall know the land that you have rejected" (Numbers 14:31).

The generation who rebelled against the Lord's Plan failed to believe the Lord and trust Him. They had forgotten the presence of His glory with them and the protection He afforded them day and night. It reminded me of the significant

1. Getting Started

words of Scripture (Luke 9:57-62) that the costs of discipleship must be met by the follower of Jesus Christ. Jesus reminded His disciples and other followers, "No one who puts his hand to the plow and looks back is fit for the kingdom of God." The emphasis of the Lord is that the follower must not look back but let go of those memories and relationships and become focused on Jesus Christ and His perfect will for him. Joshua and Caleb made this decision to follow the Lord – and – were successful. The ten spies who spread their misgivings and negatives – failed and died in the wilderness along with the people who looked back to Egypt.

In 1882, Ralph E. Hudson penned the words to a hymn that could serve as a prayer of commitment for today's follower of the Lord.

My life, my love I give to Thee,
Thou Lamb of God who died for me;
O may I ever faithful be,
My Savior and my God!

Refrain:

I'll live for Him who died for me,
How happy then my life shall be!
I'll live for Him who died for me,
My Savior and my God!

2. Fail-Safe

The term "fail-safe" has various uses, meanings and applications. The definition used in this chapter is in the noun form and means: "unlikely to fail; foolproof." An illustration is found in the preparation for the movie Apollo 13. The screenwriters had questions such as: "What are the people in Mission Control really like?" And, "Weren't there times when everybody, or at least a few people, just panicked?" The answer they received was: "No. When bad things happened, we just calmly laid out all the options, and failure was not one of them."

When applied to spiritual commitments and obligations, the idea conveyed is that failure is never an option when God's plan is being executed and His Word and guideline is fully embraced. Over the years, different servants of the Lord confidently expressed: "I am immortal until my work on this earth is done" (John Wesley). This statement was also expressed by Hudson Taylor, missionary to China; and George Whitefield, a British Evangelist who, in 1740, traveled to North America and preached a series of revivals that contributed to the Great Awakening.

The Apostle Paul reached a point in His life where he sensed a measure of invincibility in the task assigned to him by the Lord. He would boldly state: "I can do all things through Christ who gives me strength" (Philippians 4:13). Peter also expressed that the divine power of God in him equipped him so he could do all things by that power as he faithfully served the Lord (Second Peter 1:3-4).

When Joshua was being prepared to assume the leadership responsibility of completing Moses's task of bringing God's people safely into The Promised Land, he was not only being commissioned with a great task, he was also assured by the

Lord that he would be successful if he did God's work – God's way. That which the Lord had in mind for His people and His chosen leader, Joshua, is carefully spelled out in His commissioning statement to him – Joshua 1:1-9. The Lord assured Joshua that he will be successful and failure is not an option. The Lord stated: "Every place that the sole of your foot will tread upon I have given to you, just as I promised Moses" (Verse 3). The Lord added: "No man shall be able to stand before you all the days of your life…I will be with you. I will not leave or forsake you" (Verse 5).

How will Joshua be successful? What does it take to be approved by God and given His fail-safe promise? The terms and conditions of his commissioning are succinct and unamendable: "Only be strong and very courageous, being careful to do according to all the law that Moses my servant commanded you. Do not turn from it to the right hand or to the left, that you may have good success wherever you go" (Verse 8). The words of the Lord were encouraging and served to motivate Joshua to strive to please the Lord at all times and in all ways.

There are interesting differences between Moses and Joshua and their acceptance of the leadership position. When the Lord appeared to Moses and told him that he was the man to lead God's people out of the place of hostility and bondage, Moses responded with excuses of why he was the wrong choice. Just imagine the scope of this – that a man, Moses – would dare to tell God that He was making a mistake. Even though the Lord demonstrated that Moses was His man, he was still reluctant to take on that task.

Joshua represented a younger generation. It was Joshua and Caleb who were noteworthy because they followed the Lord wholeheartedly. Joshua was a military-minded person who readily acknowledged the line of command. If the Lord said he was the man, then he would do his dead-level best to accomplish the task assigned to him. Being wholehearted means: "Done or acted upon (immediately), with total sincerity, enthusiasm and commitment." When establishing the parameters for discipleship in Luke 9:62 and Luke 14:25-35, Jesus clearly stated the expectation that will qualify one to be His disciple. God does not change from His plans and purposes from one generation to another. What He required of Moses and Joshua, He requires of you and me today. He doesn't want our human rationale or excuses. He wants our commitment and compliance.

It almost seems that we believe everything that can be done or will be done depends upon us – our abilities and strategies. As a result, the Lord's work begins to be done in man's way instead of by an old principle: "God's work done in God's way will always have God's support." The work of the Lord in communities across the nation is becoming more and more dormant. One of the sad reminders of this is in the community where we reside where there are multiple road-signs about a particular denominational church. If one follows those signs, they will arrive at a lovely facility that has on its outside sign not a word of welcome or schedule of services but just one word – CLOSED.

We need to return to the basics. One of the principles God stated and means is Proverbs 16:3 (NLT): "Commit to the Lord whatever you do and your plans will succeed." This is God's fail-safe guarantee to His people in all generations

3. Good Courage

Throughout human history, there have been many instances and examples of courage being displayed during times of disruption, confrontation and combat. The basic definition of courage is: "The quality of mind and/or spirit that enables a person to face difficulty, danger or pain without fear; one who displays bravery." The British Dictionary adds: "The courage of one's convictions; the confidence to act in accordance with one's beliefs." Courage will allow one not just to opine about matters at hand but to take a stand and act in terms of that which is both true and right. There is no delay factor allowed when right and wrong – life and death – moving forward or standing still - are critical matters that demand a decision and action.

When Moses sent out the 12 spies to assess the land of Canaan, he gave them a simple directive (Numbers 13:17-20): "Go up into the Negeb and go up into the hill country, and see what the land is, and whether the people who dwell in it are strong or weak, whether they are few or many, and whether the land that they dwell in is good or bad, and whether the cities that they dwell in are camps or strongholds, and whether the land is rich or poor, and whether there are trees in it or not. Be of good courage and bring some of the fruit of the land." Take note of the Benediction with which Moses sent them: "Be of good courage." After a forty-day journey throughout the land of Canaan, the twelve spies return and are eager to give Moses, Aaron and the people of Israel their report.

They begin with a very positive report (Numbers 13:25-27). They had brought back luxurious fruit from the land. However, ten of the spies abruptly shifted from their very positive and hope-filled assessment to a very negative and despair-laden observation about fortified-cities, large and strong people, and the impossibility of possessing the land that has been promised to them (Numbers 13:28-28).

At that moment, when the people had become distressed, worried and disappointed, a person of courage emerges and takes a stand against the majority. That person was Caleb. Numbers 13:30 indicates that he did three important things at that moment in time: (1) He managed to assert himself in such a way that he was able to quiet the people; (2) Although he was a minority of one addressing the people, he encouraged them with his words, "Let us go up at once and occupy it"; and (3) He spoke words of confidence that "we are well able to overcome it." His confidence and courage was not based upon some psychological dynamic. He had the courage and was confident because of his unwavering conviction that the Lord Himself was in their midst. He was their strength and shield. He would gain the victory for them as they encountered and faced the challenges before them. He also was unwavering in his life long commitment that he would follow the Lord faithfully and wholeheartedly.

In Numbers 14:7-9, Joshua and Caleb urge the people to be confident in the Lord and the strength of His might, to avoid yielding to their fears and to stop their rebellion against the Lord and His plan for His people. This directive included that the people must have a renewed respect and confidence in their God, their appointed leaders (Moses and Aaron) along with Joshua and Caleb. The people were unconvinced and murmured and complained about their situation and concluded that their only alternative would be to: (a) replace their leaders, and (b) return to the land of Egypt (the place of hardship and intense slavery).

Would the people listen and become convinced that the Lord was on their side and would go before them and guard and keep them; and enable them to conquer and possess the land? The obvious answer is, No! Have you wondered about who was in mind in the words of Hebrews 4:2, "For good news came to us just as to them, but the message they heard did not benefit them, because they were not united by faith with those who listened." There is a distinction being drawn between those who listen and hear as opposed to those who listen, hear and believe and act positively upon that which they have listened to and heard. The NKJV clarifies the contrast and issue when it translated the words: "not being mixed with faith in those who heard it." Who are those who listened but failed to mix with faith that which had been heard?

The answer is given in Hebrews 3:16-19. "For who were those who heard and yet rebelled? Was it not all those who left Egypt led by Moses? And with whom was he provoked for forty years? Was it not with those who sinned, whose bodies fell in the wilderness? And to whom did he swear that they would not enter his rest, but to those who were disobedient? So we see that they were unable to enter because of unbelief."

The important principle regarding faith both then and now is clearly indicated in Romans 10:17, "Faith comes by hearing, and hearing by the word of God." The professing Christian needs to do a personal evaluation of his/her spiritual status before the eternal and holy God. Do I merely listen to, hear or read the Bible or do I literally believe that it is the only infallible rule for faith and practice for my life? Does the professing Christian share the commitment of Caleb that he/she is faithfully and wholeheartedly committed to God and God alone? One must "mix with faith" that which is being read (The Word of God) and heard (from those who are called to make known the whole counsel of God - Acts 20:27).

4. Unmixed

The previous chapter referenced Hebrews 4:2 regarding those who refused to incorporate faith with that which they had heard. A decision reached in rebellion or anger can and will always be accompanied with consequences. We could weary ourselves with any number of "IF Only" or "What If" thoughts and questions. IF ONLY they had given more consideration to what was behind them and the personal costs in going back to Egypt! IF ONLY they had thought about their children and the fears they had about going forward versus the uncertainty of going backward. IF ONLY they had given more thought to a God appointed leader versus their mob-mentality choice of a leader. Who would they choose to follow? How long would it be before they were displeased again with the direction they were going?

These were a people marked by fear and apprehension. They lacked faith in God and confidence in His leaders. Moses may have been on the verge of telling God – "This is why I didn't want this job when you were persuading me to do it" (Exodus 3). When faith becomes fractured or is absent, all kinds of foolish thoughts can occur and misdirection will result. The actions of Moses. Aaron, Joshua and Caleb – rent garments, sorrowing, pleading to God for the angry and disappointed people – all a sign of humility before God – served little or no positive purpose with the people UNTIL – God spoke His Word to the people. It would not be a Word that would satisfy anyone – (1) they would not be permitted to go backward to Egypt; (2) they would not be allowed to go forward to Canaan – The Promised Land; (3) they would not enjoy the luxurious fruit and product of their inheritance; (4) They would all die in the wilderness EXCEPT Joshua and

Caleb, and the little ones of the rebellious people (Numbers 14:30-35).

There is one other area for the rebellious people to reflect upon. The spies had searched out Canaan for 40 days. Because of their evil report and the rebellion of the people who believed them rather than the Lord, they would now have to wander in the wilderness for 40 years – one year for each day of the spies' journey. There is always a consequence for those who listen to God's Word but who fail to mix His Word with faith so that they incorporate it and believe it as the mandate for their lifestyle.

Another factor that the people failed to consider when they embraced an "unmixed faith" lifestyle was the dietary options they could have had versus their current food choices. God was gracious in providing Manna and Water for the rebellious people. Surely, some of them, maybe most of them would think about and reminisce with each other about the land of milk and honey, and other luxurious fruit and food they had ignored in their moment of fear and grumbling. The Lord had never promised the people a new land that was free of challenges. He told them about Canaan – a land of Promise – where they would live and rear their children in a place of fulfillment and hope. Their grumbling and rebellion short-circuited all of that because they embraced fear rather than faith. We can do similarly if we allow unguarded moments and neglect the divine promises of God to His people. It would have served them well if they had been able to sing the words attributed to Charles Wesley:

"Faith, mighty faith, the promise sees, and looks to God alone; Laughs at impossibilities, and cries: it shall be done."

What things or issues in life cause you to become hesitant in terms of your faith? Do you think or believe there are issues and things too insignificant and small for the care of God? If, or when, such moments arise in your life, what word from God should be recalled and recited by you? Do you believe He is able to do more than you can ask, think or imagine (Ephesians 3:20)? Do you believe the promises of God to His people who were living amid adverse, difficult and life-threatening circumstances (II Peter 1:3-4)? In both this passage and Ephesians 3:20, reference is made to God's power that is in you. Do you reckon with that power in or during your adverse or challenging circumstances? What about the promises of God? Which promises of God would you like to know and utilize? Does that really matter in light of Second Corinthians 1:20? Question: What does this verse tell us about the all promises of God? Answer: "They are Yes in and through Jesus Christ.

The children of Israel in their wilderness journey doubtlessly recalled God's faithfulness and goodness. As one by one the people began to die, they would wonder about their own demise in a no-man's terrain – the wilderness. Their children would be instructed that after a while they would inherit that which their parents had so foolishly rebelled against. The wise parents would be instructing their children about the folly of embracing fear rather than faith. They would include the teaching for their children to trust in the Lord with all their heart, and not lean to their own understanding. In all their ways to acknowledge the Lord and know His guidance for the paths they should take (Proverbs 3:5-6).

Meanwhile, there would be the daily journey. There would be challenges to overcome and enemies to defeat. It would be invaluable for the older generation to leave a legacy to their little ones, that the battle is not yours but the Lord's and He will never forsake His own.

5. Adjustments

The choice the majority of the Israelites made to rebel against God and His plan for them resulted in their need to adjust to a new way of life in the wilderness which was a confined and restricted area. Their wilderness home was in the form of a triangle of approximately 1500 square miles. It is a barren place without a river and with limited vegetation. The area North to South is approximately 250 miles and at its broadest east to west point is close to 150 miles. Exodus 15:22 refers to the western part as the wilderness of Shur and the eastern portion the wilderness of Paran. The wilderness area is described as being a great limestone plateau. It was bordered on the east by the valley of the Arabah, which runs from the Dead Sea to the head of the eastern branch of the Red Sea. On the south and south west were the granite mountains of Sinai and on the north the Mediterranean Sea and the mountainous region south of Judea.

If the estimate is correct, there were as many as six hundred thousand men plus women and children (Numbers 11:21) milling about in this area along with their flocks and herds. When the reality set in that the wilderness is where they would have to reside, their logical and natural concern would be: "If this is where we are to live out our lives, what will we eat; what will we drink; what will we do for clothing?" This was a similar concerned addressed by Jesus Christ in the Sermon on the Mount (Matthew 6:25-34). Jesus instructed that His people should not worry or be anxious about these necessities of life. The Lord was not unprepared for their wilderness existence, nor is He unprepared to meet your needs. He had determined that they would be nourished by a special meal from heaven each day and their thirst would be quenched with water flowing from a rock. Their heavenly meal was Manna. In the minds of the people, that word meant: "What is it?"

The people were not only resistant to the positive report about The Promised Land, they also objected to the same food supply day after day. When the dew fell upon the camp every night, God's manna fell with it. The people persisted in uttering that if they had remained in Egypt they could be eating leaks and onions rather than this monotonous manna "stuff" day after day. The malcontents among them had a propensity to complain about many things. A description of the complaints is given in Numbers 11:4-9. The text indicates the following: (1) the rabble that was among them had a strong craving. (2) the people of Israel also wept again and said, Oh that we had meat to eat! They rehearsed: "We remember the fish we ate in Egypt that cost nothing, the cucumbers, the melons, the leeks, the onions, and the garlic." (3) But now our strength is dried up, and there is nothing at all but this manna ("this God-provision") to look at. Those who had decided to make the best of their challenging situation gathered the manna and ground it. They made cakes out of it and boiled it in water.

How will the Lord handle the malcontents and camp rabble? The Lord speaks with Moses and 70 men selected by him: "You will say to the people: Consecrate yourselves for tomorrow, and you shall eat meat, for you have wept in the hearing of the Lord, saying: Who will give us meat to eat? For it was better for us in Egypt" (Numbers 11:18-20). One would think that by now the people would have begun to grow spiritually in their walk with the Lord. What was their problem? Answer: They still had a rebellious heart and a strong desire for what was behind them – Egypt, rather than a submission to the Lord's authority and what He intended for them – their very own Promised Land.

The Lord reveals His decision for the people: "The Lord will give you meat, and you shall eat. You shall not eat just one day, or two days, or five days, or ten days, or twenty days, but a whole month, until it comes out at your nostrils and becomes loathsome to you, because you have rejected the Lord who is among you and have wept before him, saying: Why did we come out of Egypt?"

When one looks at the landscape of the Church today, there are some glaring similarities with the children of Israel and their responses to the unknown and their refusal to "mix with faith" (Hebrews 4:2) that which Jesus Christ has instructed His people to be and do. Many churches are land-locked into where they have always been and how they have always functioned. They refuse to accept the reality of the demographic shifts that are occurring all-around them. There is a determination to do and have it their way rather than seeking the Lord's plan for them. As a result, a hospice-type mentality sets in and the group slowly diminishes in numbers and ministry. They have become maintenance ministries choosing to hold the hand and comfort those who will soon die off. They have chosen this rather than being the bright light that pierces the darkness and penetrates into the heart and soul of people who are lost in the darkness of their lives and culture.

I believe the Head of the Church, Jesus Christ, stands at the threshold of His Church and asks the people to let Him into their lives and Church. Sadly, He is met by the rabble and malcontents who drown out the heart-cry of those who want to be in the presence of Jesus Christ – doing God's work in God's way knowing God's blessing and His faithful provision(s). Will you make the adjustment to do and be all of what Jesus Christ wants you to do and be? He wants to guide you victoriously in the Promised Land He has prepared for you (John 14:1-3).

6. Severity

   At the time of their expressed rebellion about the prospects of challenges in The Promised Land, the people were unaware that their sojourn in the wilderness would last almost forty years. They soon learned that for the 40 days of the spies going throughout Canaan, that they would have to wander in the wilderness for forty years (one year for each day). Later they rebelled because of their dislike of Manna every day. The Lord told them they would have meat. Moses was always a man with questions regarding "how" the Lord would do something rather than accepting the fact that if God said it He will do it. Moses asked two practical, but very human, questions of the Lord (Numbers 11:22): (1) Would there be enough meat if all the flocks and herds were slaughtered for them? (2) Would they have enough meat if all the fish in the sea were caught for them?

   The Lord is not slow to answer. He might've rebuked Moses and asked Him: "Why is it that you always have to ask whether or not I can do the impossible? Is there anything too hard for me to do?" This is similar to a question raised by Jeremiah that received God's similar response (Jeremiah 32:26-27): "I am the Lord, the God of all mankind. Is anything too hard for me?" In Numbers 11:23, the Lord responds to Moses: "Is the Lord's arm too short? Now you will see whether or not what I say will come true for you."

   The Lord answers, by not only providing the desired meat, but with severe consequences as well. The response of the Lord is in Numbers 11:31-34. The Lord caused a strong wind to blow and it drove quail in from the sea. It scattered them up to two cubits (approximately 3 feet high). The people went out all day long to gather the quail and spread them about the camp. In verses 33-34 is it almost seems as though the Lord was saying: So – you wanted meat and now you have it! However, the text indicates: 'While the meat was still between their teeth and before it could be consumed, the anger of the Lord burned against the people and he struck them with a severe plague." The moment of reckoning is upon them. The Lord will be The Lord always. If He is not Lord of all, His power and glory will not be realized by the people. Why did God respond with severity? Verse 34 gives the response: The people had been slain because they rebelled and craved other food. They were not satisfied with the Lord's provision of Manna for them.

There is a marked difference between the judgments of God and the discipline of God. Numbers 11 begins with an example of the severity of God and ends with the finality of the judgment that he enacts. In verse one is a summary statement that was all too typical about the people: "Soon the people began to complain about their hardship in the hearing of the Lord, and when He heard them, His anger was kindled, and fire from the Lord blazed among them and consumed the outskirts of the camp." The idea of "fire" would serve as a warning about the power of God. The people were put on notice to alter their behavior and to cease their complaints. Otherwise, the fire would consume and purge the complainers and rebellious from the camp.

In verses 33-34, the severity of God's judgment is manifested when the rebellious malcontents had complained about the provision of God and expressed their desire for meat. The text is graphic as it states that while the meat was still between their teeth and not yet chewed, the Lord struck them down with a severe plague and the people were buried there because they craved meat rather than God's manna.

Judgment from God will always have the severity factor aligned with it whereas the discipline of God is always in the context of love, compassion and tenderness. This is indicated in Proverbs 3:12, "The Lord reproves (disciplines) those whom he loves, as a father does with the son in whom he delights." Hebrews 12:4-11 gives a well-defined fact about discipline and what it is designed to accomplish. Some of the factors mentioned are (1) the love that is being shown, (2) the correction of behavior that needs to occur, (3) it underscores the legitimacy of relationship, (4) its goal is for the good of the one being disciplined, and (5) it is to produce the harvest of righteousness and peace for those who have been diligently trained by it and been responsive to it.

Despite the rebellion of the rabble and malcontents, there is an important statement made about the character of God toward an erring people - He is longsuffering. Numbers 14:18 is the reminder that the Lord is slow to anger and abounding in steadfast love. He will forgive the iniquity and transgression of any repentant person. However, the Lord will by no means clear the guilty or non-repentant. The consequence for continuing in iniquity and transgression by the fathers will result in the displeasure of God being visited upon the children to the third and the fourth generations.

The love and compassion of God shows that He is eager to forgive and to cleanse. The justice, holiness and righteousness of God needs to be satisfied for the guilty and non-repentant. Jesus Christ fulfilled that demand for the satisfaction of a Holy God by His death on the cross – the sacrifice once for all sin. The person who seeks forgiveness and cleansing must come to Jesus Christ. It is through Christ alone that one is delivered from the severest and final judgment of God upon the sin and sinner. The Gospel Message is summarized in John 3:36, "Whoever believes in the Son has eternal life; whoever does not obey the Son shall not see life, but the wrath of God remains on him."

7. Discipline

To reach the Lord's desired goal(s) for us, the lessons learned by loving discipline must be become obvious. In other words, the pattern of one's behavior shows positive changes and the need for similar discipline diminishes. Discipline is never punitive but it is always instructive and intended to result in one's restraint. Psalm 103:8-18 tells us that God's compassion and discipline is understood by the example of the father who has compassion on his children. The Lord will have compassion on those who fear him (those who reverence Him and respond affirmatively to His Word. He knows one's needs as well as the propensity to excuse one's behavior by not applying His Word. He knows how we are formed because He made us.

As the previous chapters recounted the behavior of the rabble-rousers and malcontents, I kept thinking about Joshua and Caleb. Why were they special men who had the reputation and character of being faithful and following the Lord wholeheartedly? We don't know much about their family background like we do about Timothy or Samuel or David or Joseph.

What made Joshua and Caleb so uniquely different within a culture of people who seemed to favor captivity and slavery rather than the hope of and deliverance to The Promised Land? How had they been trained by their parents and godly people so that they were known as two men who followed the Lord wholeheartedly? Somewhere along the way, both men had received instruction about the compassion of the Lord and the benefit in complying with His directives. They would have been taught that they should embrace the positives about God and His compassion so that they would not be overwhelmed if or when negative circumstances occurred and confronted them. They would instinctively know that God is Sovereign; that His love for them was unwavering; and they would gain holiness and righteousness as they remained totally committed to Him. That alone would've given them occasion to rejoice and to be thankful to the Faithful Lord. They also witnessed the miracles God had performed in behalf of His people – the pillar of fire, the cloud leading them, water from rocks, manna from heaven, the parting of the Red Sea. They'd seen God up front and personal and had not forgotten the lessons that God was involved in the minute details of their life – big and small. These events and others would've had a significant impact on their lives.

Discipline should not always be construed negatively such as spanking, time out, sitting in a corner for a period of time, etc. Most usually think of discipline with the words of the third definition usage of the word: "punishment inflicted by way of correction and training." However, discipline also means: "the activity, exercise, or a regimen that develops or improves a skill; training." It is also described as: "training to act in accordance with basic rules; drill (rehearsing what those rules and/or principles are)"

Children rarely appreciate that some discipline administered by the parent or authority figure will be useful to them later in their life. When we think of young Israelite men such as Daniel, Hananiah, Mishaal and Azariah (Shadrach, Meshach, Abednego) who were subjected to Babylonian societal requirements and cultural values, what caused them to be courageous and uncompromising in terms of their core values and foundational principles about God and His Word? One can rightly conclude they had been well-grounded in God's Word in their respective homes. When the moment came for a choice to be made between the eternal God or the Babylonian gods and dietary codes their uncompromising choice was The Only True God regardless of the cultural (or societal) pressure applied or cost demanded.

The story of Daniel and his friends illustrate why parents should be diligent to train their children in the way they should go. Proverbs 22:5 gives one major reason why it should be faithfully done: (NIV) "In the paths of the wicked are snares and pitfalls, but those who would preserve their life stay far from them." (NLT) "Corrupt people walk a thorny, treacherous road; whoever values life will avoid it." (MSG) "The perverse travel a dangerous road, potholed and mud-slick; if you know what's good for you, stay clear of it." Because of these reasons and realities, Proverbs 22:6 must have the highest priority for a family: (NIV) "Start children off on the way they should go, and even when they are old they will not turn from it." (NLT) "Direct your children onto the right path, and when they are older, they will not leave it." (MSG) "Point your kids in the right direction—when they're old they won't be lost." To raise a godly generation will require this parental discipline. Think about these things – and – implement them as quickly as you can. There is no time to waste in the cultural malaise and influences that are prevailing in the nation and world today. God is faithful in what He will do in and for your children BUT it requires the parent being faithful and diligent in directing their children in the right path they should go.

8. Complicity

Child Psychologists and other counsellors have varied viewpoints about tough love and the application of it in the life of a difficult child or children. What exactly is Tough Love? The general meaning is: "The promotion of a person's welfare, especially that of an addict, child, or criminal, by enforcing certain constraints on them, or requiring them to take responsibility for their actions." The phrase, tough love, is believed to have originated from a book title using those words in 1968. The principles in the book have gotten wide usage as parents attempt to train their children in the right ways of the Lord.

There are two illustrations that stand out in my mind about the training of a child in the right way and how a Mother and Father became complicit in condoning misbehavior. The first example pertains to a mother and father – Rebekah and Isaac. Isaac was getting older and more feeble and he called his firstborn son, Esau, to share a personal concern and request. Isaac said to Esau, Genesis 27:2-4, "Behold, I am old; I do not know the day of my death. Now then, take your weapons, your quiver and your bow, and go out to the field and hunt game for me, and prepare for me delicious food, such as I love, and bring it to me so that I may eat, that my soul may bless you before I die." Rebekah overheard the expressed desire of Isaac but decided the second born son, Jacob, should be the recipient of the blessing of Isaac. In Genesis 27:5-17, Rebekah developed a scheme that will deceive Isaac and allow Jacob to receive Esau's blessing.

When Esau returns and approaches his father, the deception is revealed. In Genesis 27:34-36, Esau is offended, hurt and outraged. He says to his father: "(Jacob) has cheated me these two times. He took away my birthright, and behold, now he has taken away my blessing." He goes on to plead with his father for a special blessing for himself. If Rebekah had not been complicit with Jacob in the deception of Isaac, much difficulty and division would've been avoided. Rather than scheming to deceive, Rebekah needed to exercise a form of tough love with Jacob. She could not do so because of the scheme she devised to deceive her husband, Jacob' father.

The second example is in Luke 15, Jesus' Parable of the Prodigal Son. Luke 15:11-12 gives the basic premise: Jesus said, "There was a man who had two sons. And the younger of them said to his father: Father, give me the share of property that is coming to me." Without any discussion or statement of resistance, the father complies with his son's request (more of a demand). Was the father afraid of the son? Did he fear some severe action/reaction if he refused to do so? The fact that he complied allowed the community where he lived to come up with varied opinions and draw all kinds of false conclusions. One fact is that the man divided his estate between his two sons. In doing so, he lost his influence in and the esteem of the community where he resided. What if the father had applied Tough Love with the younger son rather than listlessly going along with his demands? What if the father had said, No? What if he had told this erstwhile son that he had not earned the right to make such a demand at that time? What does he think the recourse would've been on the part of the son?

So often, a parent can miscalculate the reaction of a child or some other person and fail to stand upon the core values and foundational principles established by the Lord. The son took all of his demanded possessions and went off to a far country. Presumably, it was as far away as possible from his father and home. The parable is well known and we learned that the son squandered all of his possessions. He was friendless and alone. He took a job where he became a type of slave that fed a farmer's hogs. He was so hungry that he even ate some of the "slop" that was intended for the pigs. At that point of helplessness and despair, he decided to return home and offer himself to be a servant/slave for his father.

He had no idea what his reception will be. He didn't know whether the father had been looking down the road every day to see if/when his younger son would return home. The son worked on a speech of repentance. When the father saw his son shuffling towards home he ran to him. He had his servants clothe him with clean garments, a robe and a ring. He orders a party because the son who had been lost was now found and back home where there was a safe place of refuge and care for him.

Should the father have responded in this way? Should he set up rules and regulations – pro and con - by which this son should now live? Would everyone commend the father for what he was doing and the party he was throwing for his younger son? The older brother complained and would not attend the party. The father went to him to plead that he come to the celebration. The older son was adamant. Doubtlessly, other people in the community disagreed with the father's response. They chose to neither hug the returning son nor the father. They refused to come to the party.

Jesus would have us apply this parable to our own lives, actions and reactions. Would you hug the returning sinner? Would you hug the gracious father? Would you attend the party that celebrated that which had been lost and has now been found? Jesus wants us to reevaluate what a Biblical Church and a Biblical Christian should be eager to do. Are you hesitant to embrace in Jesus' name the one who is dirty, smelly, ragged, hopeless and helpless? Jesus would want us to answer these questions truthfully before Him. He already knows the answer. He just wants us to be honest with Him as well as with ourselves. He wants us to be willing in act in His behalf and in His name.

A lesson to be learned from these two family situations is that God had declared His values for a husband and wife, as well as for parents and children. When these values are ignored, there is diversity and breakdown in relationships. There will also be latent but recurring consequences because of one's neglect of God's family values.

Obviously, Rebecca erred in developing a scheme to deceive her husband and to gain a beneficial advantage for Jacob. She was complicit in that which was evil and there was conflict in the family from that point onward. The father of the prodigal son should've been firm in family values rather than complying with a younger son's demand. The father had no idea what the son with do with his share of the estate. He knew when he saw his bedraggled son shuffling down the path toward the home he had been anxious to leave. When the father erred earlier, it resulted in sibling rivalry and jealousy. The first question from the older brother illustrates the jealousy: "How come you never had a party and all the invited guests from the community for me?" In both cases, Rebecca and Jacob, and the father and his returning son illustrated parental failure in training the children adequately. Parents must be principled and strong in their training of the children, and children must obey their parents and learn godliness and righteousness from them.

9. Tough Love

Proverbs 22 – contains the words about training up one's child (Vs. 5-6). There are any number of people in the Bible where little is specifically known about how they were reared. Some that readily come to mind are – Joshua and Caleb; Daniel, Hananiah, Mishaal and Azariah; several of the Prophets, etc. All we know is that they were trained in the way they should go and chose to consistently live that way throughout their adult years.

Proverbs 22 also makes reference to the time and place for corporal punishment/discipline. Corporal Punishment has as one of its definitions: "physical punishment, such as a spanking that is inflicted on a child by an adult in authority." The reasoning for Biblical Corporal Punishment is based on the following words of wisdom in Proverbs 22:15: "Foolishness is bound up in the heart of a child; the rod of discipline [correction administered with godly wisdom and lovingkindness] will remove it far from him." Proverbs 29:15 echoes a similar observation and instruction (ESV): "The rod and reproof give wisdom, but a child left to himself brings shame to his mother." There is a further statement about physical or corporal discipline in Proverbs 23:12-14 (ESV), "Apply your heart to instruction and your ear to words of knowledge. Do not withhold discipline from a child; if you strike him with a rod, he will not die. If you strike him with the rod, you will save his soul from Sheol (death/hell)." These words provide instruction and a more complete perspective of that which The Lord expresses in His Word about a form of corporal punishment/discipline.

This instruction and perspective must also be considered with a required Scriptural balance. Ephesians 6:1-4 reminds parents (and fathers in particular): "Children, obey your parents in the Lord, for this is right. Honor your father and mother (this is the first commandment with a promise), that it may go well with you and that you may live long in the land. Fathers, do not provoke your children to anger, but bring them up in the discipline and instruction of the Lord." Fathers are to be focused on the discipline and instruction of the Lord. An important passage that gives a practical application of this duty and responsibility is the instruction in Exodus 12:26-27, "When a child (son) shall ask what the Passover ceremony means, the father shall instruct him." The Lord's Supper should be emphasized in a similar way.

Joshua 4:21-24 is an equally powerful illustration about the instruction of the Lord to His people as he brought them into The Promised Land. The Memorial Stones carried from the riverbed of the Jordan River were to remind the people how they got to where they were and who intervened in their behalf to get them there. The concept of a father giving instruction to his children is underscored in First Thessalonians 2:11-12, "For you know how, like a father with his children, we exhorted each one of you and encouraged you and charged you to walk in a manner worthy of God, who calls you into his own kingdom and glory."

None of the instruction connected to discipline should be construed as negating a time and place where spanking would be appropriate. In the modern religious culture, there are many varied opinions regarding the application of physical discipline. Proverbs 22:15 is frowned upon because of what it states as a means for correction: (NLT) "A youngster's heart is filled with foolishness, but physical discipline will drive it far away." These things are shared so you will have a more complete perspective of that which The Lord expresses in His Word about a form of discipline. One must be careful with a definition for the word "rod". There is a wide difference between a switch (a small, thin twig from a shrub) and a Table Leg (or a 2 X 2 piece of lumber). As Biblical discipline is administered, Psalm 103:13-14 must be one's guideline: "As a father shows compassion to his children, so the Lord shows compassion to those who fear him. For he knows our frame (body structure and its frailty); He remembers how He created us - that we are dust."

A spanking, when needed, can and should be administrated along with counsel and instruction. If it is a beating administered to a child every day on the premise that he/she must've done something wrong and deserved it – that is an erroneous premise and a non-Biblical approach and purpose. Following God's Word precisely can be challenging and difficult. If a spanking becomes necessary, the child must always be aware of the parent's love and compassion for them. It is the hope of a Biblical parent that the child will not repeat wrong behavior that requires correction. The spiritual objective is that the children will learn and desire to follow the Lord faithfully and wholeheartedly.

May God grant each of us the needed wisdom that we will love our children and their children, and desire only the very best blessing of a gracious God to each of them.

10. Adaptation

In life, there are always occasions when one must adapt to a new set of circumstances. Failure to do so will cause one to become immobilized and miss the God-ordained opportunities and responsibilities. The Apostle Paul shared his personal guiding principle about adapting. In First Corinthians 9:19-23, he summarizes his flexibility in ministry by stating that he never lost sight of his goal and commitment of becoming all things to all people in order that some will receive the Gospel – Jesus Christ – and be saved. He was emphatic and underscored his reason by saying "I do all of this for the sake of the Gospel."

Paul had another guiding principle whose premise is shared in a simple Christian song: "I have decided to follow Jesus...No turning back." Looking constantly into the rear-view mirror of a vehicle will cause dangerous situations ahead. It is vital to pay attention to where one is; where one is going; and the best way to reach that destination. In part, it is what Paul wrote in Philippians 3:13, "Forgetting what is behind and exerting myself to what is ahead, I press on toward the goal..."

It would have been so easy for Joshua and Caleb to harbor resentment toward the ten spies who presented a negative report about the promised land. The spies and their report discouraged and disheartened a generation of people. In like manner, it caused grumbling and opposition toward Moses and Aaron, along with Joshua and Caleb. If Moses, Aaron, Joshua and Caleb had been resentful towards these ten men and the people who were persuaded by them, they would've missed out on God's plan and provision for them. God took care of the ten negative spies and they died. God also took care of the rebellious generation and they all died in the wilderness. After the decision had been made by the Lord that the rebellious people would never enter the Promised Land, there was considerable work that needed to be done. This work would require patience and diligence, especially for Joshua and Caleb. They were the aides/attendants of Moses and Aaron who would prepare the next generation for the moment when they would enter Canaan – The Promised Land. This time of preparation would entail a waiting period of thirty-eight to forty years before the Jordan River would be crossed and the Promised Land entered. Joshua and Caleb would be the key leaders for the younger generation as they moved forward. They would organize and prepare them for the task that awaited them as they possessed the land promised by the Lord. Joshua and Caleb would've been remiss in their privilege if they merely recalled the past and the reason for this delay.

What would have to be done in the meantime? There would be battles to be fought and great lessons to be learned as Joshua led his militia-type army against formidable foes. A dramatic moment takes place in one of these conflicts. Exodus 17:8-13 records the war with the Amalekites at Rephidim. The battle will be won by Joshua and his militia – BUT – how was it accomplished against overwhelming odds? The text indicates that when Moses held his hands lifted up to the Lord, Joshua had the advantage. But when Moses' arms became weary and weak and drooped the advantage disappeared. Aaron and Hur held Moses' arms upward to the Lord and the battle was won because of the faith and confidence that the Lord would defend and protect His people.

In Exodus 17:14-16, the Lord instructs Moses: "Write this as a memorial in a book and recite it in the ears of Joshua, that I will utterly blot out the memory of Amalek from under heaven." This would serve as an incentive to keep looking ahead and pressing toward the goal. It would also suggest that trusting in the Lord is vital. One must keep on looking to the Lord for His will and strength for the journey He has assigned to His people. There will be other conflicts and other battles ahead but Joshua will never forget this moment when the strength of the Lord was sought and His deliverance took place. From the beginning, Joshua was faithful and followed the Lord wholeheartedly. He and Caleb would never be diverted from their commitment and confidence. Both men would be an example to the younger generation who would inherit the land. Their faithfulness and total commitment to God would be their legacy.

What legacy are you leaving – have you left – for the next generation? Prayerfully – consider these things and be willing to adapt to the circumstances and consequences that are part of your sphere of ministry today. You can and will be an influence. May it be that you wholeheartedly and faithfully followed the Lord all the days of your life.

11. Patience

The paths ordered by the Lord for an individual are not always easy ones. A template for one's life could easily be - Jeremiah 29:11 - where the Lord is speaking and says: "I know the plans that I have for you." The issue for each of us includes both anticipation and compliance. The basic fact is that each child of God must fit his/her life into that plan of God. This must've been very challenging for Joshua and Caleb. They had explored The Promised Land and were convinced they could and would overcome it because of the Lord's presence with them and the people. However, that would not happen in the immediate. Joshua and Caleb would have to wait thirty-eight years to realize that which they knew was possible.

For us individually and personally, it must be remembered that "my" schedule may be at variance with God's schedule. Most of us live our lives in the immediate and regularly make impulse choices and decisions. If only our lives would be lived within the parameter of the Psalmist when he wrote - Psalm 37:7 that the ambition and goal of one's life should be to "(Be still) Rest (Relax) in the Lord and wait patiently for Him." The Psalmist frequently wrote about and spoke of the need to wait for the Lord's plan to unfold and for His timing for his life. In Psalm 25:3, he wrote: "None who wait for You will be put to shame; but those who are faithless without cause will be disgraced." In Psalm 27:14, he reminded himself and us to: "Wait for the Lord; be strong, and let your heart take courage; wait for the Lord!" The whole idea of waiting, resting, relaxing and being still before the Lord doesn't seem to compute in the twenty-first culture. We live in a world of "instant" everything and it becomes easy to want to fit God into that box as well.

I so often forget the words of the prophet who reminded his generation of the great need and truth to wait, trust and hope in the faithful God. The words are in Isaiah 40:31, "They who WAIT for the Lord shall renew their strength; they shall mount up with wings like eagles; they shall run and not be weary; they shall walk and not faint" (NIV). "Those who HOPE in the Lord" (NLT). "Those who TRUST in the Lord."

What does it mean to "wait" for anyone/anything? The general definition is: "to delay temporarily." To wait or linger implies putting off further activity (or change) until later. It includes staying for a limited time for a definite purpose, usually for something expected. An encouraging reference regarding waiting for something that is expected is Habakkuk 2:3, "For the vision awaits an appointed time; it testifies of the end, and will not lie. Though it lingers, wait for it, since it will surely come and not delay." The Lord is addressing a day of severity and judgment. How did the prophet respond to the Lord's Word? How should we respond to it? The response is in Habakkuk 3:16-19. "I hear, and my body trembles…I will QUIETLY WAIT for the day of the Lord…" As he contemplated total devastation by the hand of the Lord, everything coming to ruin and being surrounded by death of all livestock, the prophet exclaims (3:18-19), "I will rejoice in the Lord; I will take joy in the God of my salvation. God, the Lord, is my strength…He makes me tread on high places."

In a Desiring God Devotional (March 2019), the writer raises the following thoughts about waiting based on Psalm 13:1-2, "How long, O Lord? Will You forget me forever? How long will you hide Your face from me? How long must I take counsel in my soul and have sorrow in my heart all the day?" The application includes two additional questions: "Does David strike a chord with you as he cries out in desperation? Is God causing an AGONIZING WAIT for answers to your most urgent and heartfelt prayers?" The writer's insights touch a nerve within most of us who have been there and had those same or similar questions. One of the nerves the questions struck in me brought to mind words from an old Hymn written by George W. Chadwick (1890):

> I sought the Lord, and afterward I knew
> He moved my soul to seek Him, seeking me.
> It was not I that found, O Savior true;
> No, I was found of Thee.

I know that I need more patience in waiting for the Lord's timing and His best plan for my life. Sometimes, I have felt pressured to act immediately rather than to consult with the Lord for His will. I have seen the startled reaction of sales personnel, and others, when I indicated to them that my wife and I had interest in a particular item or decision but we would take time to pray about it and to learn what God's will is for us and then we will let them know what decision we've reached after discussing it together and praying about before the Lord. I would advise you to do similarly. One should never let anyone else try to fit one into their box (mold).

Waiting on and for the Lord is always the best action one can take before any choice is made or decision reached. The reminder in Habakkuk 2:3 should be emblazoned in one's mind and spirit: (NLT) "The vision...wait patiently, for it will surely take place. It will not be delayed." Confidently wait on the Lord. He will never fail or disappoint you. "As for this God - His way (His will and His timing) is perfect; the word of the Lord proves true; he is a shield for all those who take refuge in him" (Psalm 18:30).

In 1851, Horatius Bonar penned words about God's will and way in one's life. My wife and I personalized the words and used it as a wedding prayer and life commitment.

James Perry

Your way, not ours, O Lord…
Lead us by Thine own hand,
Choose out the path for us.

We dare not choose our lot;
We would not, if we might;
You choose for us, our God,
So we shall walk aright.

12. Distractions

One of the tools used often by the enemy of one's soul is distraction (dividing one's attention; preventing one's attention or concentration; an interruption; mental turmoil or anger). The enemy's objective is to divert one from being focused on God and His plan for one's life. The Scriptures challenge us (Hebrews 12:2) to keep on looking to Jesus, the Author and Finisher of our faith. Some obvious distractions can be in the area of family, employment, education or general cares about life in particular and the world in general.

Luke 18:13-14 (NLT) indicates a sharp contrast in the parable of the sower and his seed. Some of the seed is described as falling among thorns. How does Jesus define some of the things he declares to be thorns in one's life? He stated: "The seeds that fell among the thorns represent those who hear the message, but all too quickly the message is crowded out by the cares and riches and pleasures of this life. And so they never grow into maturity." Every Lord's Day morning, one can observe the reality of this description – people doing yard work; boats hooked up on trailers and the anticipation of spending a day at the lake, river or gulf. Cares, riches and pleasure have crowded out remembering to worship the Lord and to fellowship with the people of God. Result: leanness of one's soul and spiritual well-being.

On the other hand, Jesus describes those who have received the seed differently: "The seeds that fell on the good soil represent honest, good-hearted people who hear God's word, cling to it, and patiently produce a huge harvest." They are the ones who are taking a serious God seriously. Result: blessing in one's life, family, employment or education. Why? Because they cherished being in the presence of the Lord and worshipping Him in spirit and truth.

Let's insert Joshua and Caleb into this parable (the seed on good soil). They had every reason to be annoyed and indifferent toward the Israelites because of their foolish and rebellious ways. They had to wander in the wilderness because of the unwise decision of the people and their rejection of God's best plan and will for their lives. Rather than looking at the rebellious generation and becoming distracted, Joshua and Caleb committed themselves to prepare the children for their ultimate entrance into the land of promise. Even though it would take an extended period of time (thirty-eight years) and an arduous journey, they kept their eyes fixed on the Lord, His plan and His will.

In one's personal life, there are times of difficulty that come and unexpected challenges where one is ill-prepared to know how to cope with them. The key is to keep focused on the Lord and being strong in the Lord and the strength of His might. Joshua and Caleb did not have the hymn writer, John Newton (1775). They nevertheless functioned in a way that demonstrate for us that they knew the truths about which Newton wrote:

Though troubles assail us and dangers affright,
though friends should all fail us and foes all unite,
yet one thing secures us, whatever betide,
The promise assures us, "The Lord will provide."

When Satan assails us to stop up our path,
and courage all fails us, we triumph by faith.
He cannot take from us, though oft he has tried,
This heart-cheering promise, "The Lord will provide."

No strength of our own and no goodness we claim;
yet, since we have known of the Savior's great name,
in this our strong tower for safety we hide:
The Lord is our power, "The Lord will provide."

12. Distractions

In Philippians 3:13-14, Paul of maintaining one's focus and exerting oneself to reach the goal, the reward awaiting in heaven for faithful and wholehearted servants of the Lord. He frames this thought in terms of spiritual maturity (3:15). He adds a further word of encouragement (3:17) to follow those who have set and established a godly example.

Joshua and Caleb set a similar example before the people of their day. While the older generation did not embrace it, their children would and did. All distractions must be relegated to the act of "forgetting what is behind" so that they are unhindered in reaching the goal that is ahead. We can and should honor such men and gladly follow their example. In doing so, we will increase our level of spiritual maturity and impact others to similarly follow our example because we are following the Lord as best and as closely as we can. If they follow us, they will be following the Lord Jesus Christ. Be aware of Paul's words – First Corinthians 11:1 – "Be imitators of me, as I am of Christ."

13. Energized

Have you ever experienced a "blah" kind of day or period of time? If you have this experience, what can you do to turn a "blah" day into a "blessing" day? There is a wide-ranging spectrum that references various philosophies for life. Some are energized to follow one lifestyle whereas others choose something different. One of the things I have observed during my lifetime is that false philosophies and false religionists have a way of captivating the mind, emotion and will of those who embrace that which is being promoted.

In the Devotional, Insight for Living, July 9, 2019, the following possible choices of a philosophy for life were listed:

The Greeks said:	Be wise, know yourself.
Rome said:	Be strong, discipline yourself.
Judaism says:	Be holy, conform yourself.
Epicureanism says:	Be sensuous, enjoy yourself.
Educationists say:	Be resourceful, expend yourself.
Psychology says:	Be confident, fulfill yourself.
Materialism says:	Be acquisitive, please yourself.
Pride says:	Be superior, promote yourself.
Asceticism says:	Be inferior, suppress yourself.
Diplomacy says:	Be reasonable, control yourself.
Communism says:	Be collective, secure yourself.
Humanism says:	Be capable, trust yourself.
Philanthropy says:	Be unselfish, give yourself.

In the midst of the children of Israel's long wilderness journey, they might've chosen one philosophy or another but soon they would become disillusioned. Joshua and Caleb made an early decision in their lives to devote all their energy and effort to follow the Lord wholeheartedly. The others did not follow in their commitment. They may have deemed Joshua and Caleb foolhardy to resolutely hold to their faith and commitment. While they did not have many of the writings of Scripture at that point, they demonstrated they had learned some invaluable basic principles of how they could best live an energized life. Seven hundred years later, Isaiah would be speaking in behalf of the Lord to some people who were similar to those in the wilderness. When Isaiah was commissioned by the Lord to do his ministry, he was told about going to a people who were stubborn in their heart and mind toward the things of God.

The Lord instructed his prophet (Isaiah 6:9-10 - NLT): "Listen carefully, but do not understand. Watch closely, but learn nothing. Harden the hearts of these people. Plug their ears and shut their eyes. That way, they will not see with their eyes, nor hear with their ears, nor understand with their hearts and turn to me for healing." It is a hopeless message. The Lord also had His prophet declare (Isaiah 40:31): "Those who trust in the Lord will find new strength. They will soar high on wings like eagles. They will run and not grow weary. They will walk and not faint." This message was one of hope. This energized Isaiah as well as the people who received and responded to it. This same principle and fact about the Lord energized both Joshua and Caleb. It motivated them to keep on keeping on even though there were challenges all along the way. They knew the Lord and knew in their souls the words later penned in Psalm 18:25, "To the faithful, You show Yourself faithful; to those with integrity (and are blameless) You show integrity (that You are blameless)."

We live in a day and time when the twenty-first century church is waning. Demographics have shifted and people have relocated. Those who desire and work to keep churches alive, in too many instances, find themselves in a similar role as the one who is trying to fill a bucket with water despite the fact that the bucket has many holes in it. It can be frustrating at best and disheartening at worst.

We need to remind ourselves of the words in Galatians 6:9 (ESV), "Let us not grow weary of doing good, for in due season we will reap, if we do not give up." One older version translates the last phrase: "If we faint not." Horatius Bonar (1843) wrote the inspiring, challenging and motivational words that should be the song of one's heart:

Go, labor on: spend, and be spent,
Thy joy to do the Father's will:
It is the way the Master went;
Should not the servant tread it still?

Go, labor on! 'tis not for naught
Thine earthly loss is heavenly gain;
Men heed thee, love thee, praise thee not;
The Master praises: what are men?

14. Darkness

When choices are selected and decisions made, one needs to be guarded in terms of why the selections were made. When done incorrectly, the mind becomes confused and the direction one should go becomes obscured. It is like walking across an unlit bridge in the darkness and being uncertain if it reaches the other side. Many people have an innate fear of darkness because there is the thought and feeling that someone or something is lurking in the darkness – something nefarious (wicked or criminal) may suddenly occur and cause one to experience a degree of horror,

Jesus Christ referenced these possibilities in John 3:19-20 (NLT), "The judgment is based on this fact: God's light came into the world, but people loved the darkness more than the light, for their actions were evil. All who do evil hate the light and refuse to go near it for fear their sins will be exposed." Not knowing who those people are who love the darkness, or when they will suddenly appear, only enhances one's fear of the unknown. Joshua and Caleb knew these were some of the innate fears of the children of Israel. They people lacked the ability to trust the Lord even in the darkest moments. One such incident occurred when the Egyptians pursued the children of Israel after they left Egypt. Moses led the people to the edge of the Red Sea. With the Egyptian army closing in from behind (Exodus 14:10-12) and the Red Sea preventing them from moving forward, it was a dark moment in the experience of the people. They complained. They were filled with fear. They argued and complained that it would've been best if they had continued in their slavery in Egypt.

How can a scared and fearful people become hopeful and believe the Lord is able to deliver them? Moses spoke to them with a clear and unequivocal declaration (Exodus 14:13-14),

"Fear not, stand firm, and see the salvation of the Lord, which he will work for you today. For the Egyptians whom you see today, you shall never see again. The Lord will fight for you, and you have only to be silent."

The people have a choice – fear and darkness, or faith and light. Will they be silent and stop their complaining? Will they believe that a miracle is about to happen so they can cross the Red Sea on dry ground? What will it take for them to believe in the available salvation from the Lord? What does it take for you to believe in the Lord for His deliverance?

Fear and darkness so easily grips one's soul. In 1874, Mary Baker wrote a hymn in which she included the words: "The sky is overshadowed with blackness, No shelter or help is nigh." In 1834, Edward More wrote the Hymn that included: "When darkness seems to hide His face..." In the 1980s, Frank Peretti wrote two books on the subject: "This Present Darkness" and "Piercing The Darkness." These books captured the interest of more than 15 million people. Terry Powell posts a Blog, "Penetrating The Darkness" and shares keen insights about depression and the darkness one can experience at such a time.

The children of Israel were recalcitrant. If only they had chosen to follow Joshua and Caleb's recommendation about The Promised Land. Their lives could've been enriched; their journey could've been without incident; and they could've inherited The Promised Land confidently and victoriously. Apart from that, the people will know a life of fear, danger, despair and complaint. They needed a new song in their hearts and souls similar to a stanza from an anthem written by L.E. Singer and Don Wyrtzen - -

FINALLY HOME
When engulfed by the terror Of tempestuous seas;
Unknown waves before you roll...
When surrounded by the blackness Of the darkest night;
O how lonely death can be..."

14. Darkness

What is available to one who is passing through the valley of the shadow of death? How did Joshua and Caleb manage to represent the light amid their surrounding of darkness? The Refrain of the anthem emboldens one's faith and confidence:

Just think of stepping on shore And finding it heaven;
Of touching a hand and finding it God's;
Of breathing new air and finding it celestial
Of waking up in glory and finding it home.

Do you have a propensity of looking at events and circumstances that inhibit your confidence rather than looking to Jesus Christ? Do you tend to let your fear blind you to faith and trust in the Lord? Do you allow yourself to look at the darkness rather than the one who is The Light? Do you view your spiritual cup as one that is half full or half empty? It cannot be both! You must trust in the Lord with ALL your heart and lean not to your own understanding. You must acknowledge the Lord in all your ways, at all times and for all things. When this is your commitment, He will lead and guide you on the best path and one of great blessing.

15. Unheralded

There seems to be quite a bit of unfairness in the culture and world. A person can be diligent and hardworking but never receive any recognition for their achievements or efforts. For the servant of the Lord, the efforts and achievements are for Him who called one into service. A very excellent verse that establishes this perspective is First Corinthians 10:31, "...Whatever you do, do it all for the glory of God."

There is a time and place for recognition and encouragement to be given. In First Thessalonians 5:11-13, we are instructed to, "Encourage one another and build one another up, just as you are doing...respect those who labor among you and are over you in the Lord and admonish you, and esteem them very highly in love because of their work."

If Joshua and Caleb had been waiting for the children of Israel to commend and encourage them, they would be sorely disappointed. The children of Israel had physically left Egypt but inwardly their hearts remained in the land of slavery and bondage. Time and time again they raised the issue of how much better off they were in Egypt than they were now in a place of uncertainty and wandering. They could not forget what they left behind and declined to look forward in faith to that which awaited them. It was more difficult for Joshua and Caleb because the people rejected their best effort to encourage them.

There is another important text about interactional encouragement of the people who are following the Lord. In Hebrews 10:24-25, the word of instruction and obligation is: "Let us consider how to stir up one another to love and good works, not neglecting to meet together, as is the habit of some, but encouraging one another, and all the more as you see The Day drawing near."

It becomes more difficult for one who has been reared in the church community nearly all of his/her life to feel they are not essential, not wanted nor heralded in any way. They seem to feel as though their faithfulness to their church community has been in vain. This is especially true within the clergy peer group. Some, who are no more worthy to be acclaimed than someone else, are given recognition and honor. There are good, faithful and humble men who have relinquished a place of ministry rather than to get into conflict over position or ministry. They have gone on to minister in other situations but they have done so with a wounded and aching heart because they are not in the place they would love to be serving. To step aside is not easy.

The irony is that the one who pushed his way into a ministering situation does so blithely without any sense of what he has done or how his actions affect others. The consolation for the one who feels pushed aside and unwanted is that he is serving the Lord who has opened another door for him. A key in the midst of all the turmoil is to keep oneself free from any degree of rancor. The ultimate consolation is that the Master and Savior Jesus Christ was pushed aside and mistreated. He was deemed to be unwanted and unneeded even though He was the Son of God and the Lamb who would be sacrificed once for all for sin. The irony is that the ones who pushed him aside could come to Him and receive eternal life from Him. An older Christian song written with a soloist in mind contains these meaningful words:

> Come, all ye weary and oppressed,
> O come and I will give you rest;
> I'll bid your anxious fears depart,
> For I am meek and lowly in heart…
> And I will give you rest.

15. Unheralded

Refrain:
> Ye that labor and are heavy-laden,
> Come, come, come,
> and learn of Me;
> My yoke is easy, My burden is light,
> and my burden is light,
> My yoke is easy, My burden is light,
> Come, O come,
> Come, and I will give you rest.

He is the only way and only hope for the lost and wandering soul. Have you come to Him and found His rest? His invitation to come is freely extended to you. Come to Him and find His rest for you.

16. Expectation

On different occasions, the Word of God addresses earnestness and expectation. Paul combined these two concepts when he wrote, Philippians 1:20-21 (NKJV), "According to my earnest expectation and hope that in nothing I shall be ashamed, but with all boldness, as always, so now also Christ will be magnified in my body, whether by life or by death. For to me, to live is Christ, and to die is gain."

Paul also emphasized "earnestness" when he wrote in Second Corinthians 8:7 (NIV), "But since you excel in everything…in complete earnestness…" Question: Does the organized Church today radiate "Earnest Expectation"? What about the genuine Biblical Church, does it display "Earnest Expectation"? If Jesus Christ appeared in a given Church today, what would His assessment be of the Church that is supposed to be His Bride? Would He be pleased with it? Would He commend it? Or – would He point out the inconsistencies between His "expectations" for it and point out the Church's drift and complacency?

There is a reason why hundreds of churches close each year. One consideration that is rarely given notice are the words of Jesus Christ to the Seven Churches in Revelation 2 and 3. The ever-present measure of Jesus for His Church is whether or not a Church remembers, returns, repents and renews according to His prescription for the purpose and mission of His Church – to know Christ and to make Him known. One area that is often overlooked is in the words Paul wrote about the gifts that were given by the Lord, as well as the purpose of those gifts, Ephesians 4:11-13. What did the Lord gift men to be and do? What was His "earnest expectation" for His Bride, the Church?

Paul wrote: "He gave the apostles, the prophets, the evangelists, the shepherd- teachers, to equip the saints (the genuine people of God) for the work of ministry, for building up the body of Christ, until we all attain to the unity of the faith and of the knowledge of the Son of God, to mature manhood, to the measure of the stature of the fullness of Christ..." Is any of this happening as Jesus Christ expressed it? Maybe to a degree but why then are congregations dwindling in size and church buildings closing?

There are no simple answers for the question. It is a combination of several diverse factors, such as – changing demographics; lack of vision and focus in terms of ministry opportunities; overall complacency; reluctance to become engaged; a resignation for the Church to survive as best it can until its resources are expended; a contentment to preserve a "legacy" by means of a maintenance type of operation; inability to be engaged in doing the work of ministry.

Dr. J. I. Packer shared a paper on the subject of Revival. In one section of that paper, he addressed the local Church: "There must be Fruitfulness In Testimony. Revival always has an evangelistic and ethical overspill into the world. When God revives the church, the new life overflows from the church for the conversion of outsiders and renovation of society. Christians become fearless in witness and tireless in their Savior's service. They proclaim by word and deed the power of the new life, souls are won, and a community conscience informed by Christian values emerges. Also in revival times God acts quickly; his work accelerates. Truth spreads, and people are born again and grow in Christ, with amazing rapidity."

Is that what you desire as a genuine Christian? Is that what the Church you attend committed to be and do? Does your "earnest expectation" square with Jesus Christ's expectation for you? Are YOU willing to step into the gap and be what

16. Expectation

God wants you, and all true believers, to be and do? If not now
– when? If not here – where?

17. Misdirection

GPS (Global Positioning System) is a helpful tool in most newer cars. It is also available in portable devices that one can utilize when travelling. There are times when these devices have not been available and one must reply on a map or instinct. However, there are times when that fails and one has gone the wrong way and doesn't have a clue of his/her location.

There was a rainy night when this occurred with my wife and me. We were on a road where we had travelled many times before. Only on this particular rainy night, at a very crucial spot, a vehicle approaching from the opposite direction had high beams on. It temporarily blinded us in terms of where we were and we missed an important turn in the road. Not knowing we had missed the turn, we continued on the road that soon was no longer paved. Very quickly, it became more and more narrow. It was dark and rainy! No lights on the road. On either side of the narrowed road were deep ditches that prevented us from being able to turn around. Additionally, there was no Mobile Phone Signal that would've allowed us to call for assistance. What should we do? What could we do?

Throughout history other people have faced a similar dilemma. In the case of the children of Israel on their journey from Egypt to The Promised Land, they made a deliberate choice to make a bad decision by following the negative input by ten of the twelve spies Moses had sent out to report on the land they were to possess. Despite the best appeal by Moses, Aaron, Joshua and Caleb, they decided to follow the misdirection placed before them in the report by ten fearful and apprehensive men.

At a different time another set of 12 men witnessed Jesus perform the miracle of the loaves which fed thousands of hungry people. Afterwards, Jesus told the disciples to get into a boat and row to the other side of the lake. Mark 6:50-52 (NLT) records the experience of the disciples on a dark, windy and rainy night, in their boat rowing as hard as they can but making no progress toward land or a safe port. Jesus comes walking across the storm-tossed waters and says to them: "Don't be afraid... Take courage! I am here! Then he climbed into the boat, and the wind stopped..." Their reaction was one of total amazement. Why? "They still didn't understand the significance of the miracle of the loaves and fishes. Their hearts were too hard to take it in."

Proverbs 14:12 reminds us that there is a way that seems right to a man and woman existing within a given culture. The choice made about that way is determinative in terms of their destination. Just because a pathway may look alright at the outset is no indicator of where it will lead. This verse concludes, "but in the end it is the way of death." As though he wishes to underscore this statement, Solomon repeated it in Proverbs 16:25. A Biblical admonition which should be emblazoned on the heart, soul and mind of every true follower of Jesus Christ is First Corinthians 16:13 (NIV), "Be on your guard; stand firm in the faith; be courageous; be strong." Heeding that admonition will enable one to stay the course and reach God's destination for you safely. Be confident and assured that God is faithful and will guard and keep you. There is no misdirection with Him.

Back to the experience my wife and I had on a very dark and rainy night. Although we felt very insecure and endangered, we prayed and then reached our decision. We would attempt to back out on that narrow dirt road with deep drainage ditches on either side. Very slowly, with only the backup lights giving illumination, my wife watched on one side and I on the other as we navigated in reverse. Finally, we came to a slight indent on that road. Carefully, I maneuvered the car and with my wife's words of caution, finally – we were

17. Misdirection

turned around and heading toward the place where I had missed our turn. We gave a sigh of relief and praise to the Lord for once again guiding, guarding and keeping us safe in His hands and under His control. A lesson we learned that night was that we never wanted to go down that road again.

Since then, we have travelled past that point again and again. Each time, we indicate that we never want to go in that direction anymore. There is a very old Hymn that contains these meaningful words:

> Though the road be rough and stormy,
> Trackless as the foaming sea,
> Thou hast trod this way before me,
> And I gladly follow Thee.

Refrain:
> I will follow Thee, my Savior,
> Thou didst shed Thy blood for me;
> And though all men should forsake Thee,
> By Thy grace I'll follow Thee.

18. Meditating

A previous chapter focused on God's law and commands that He intended as the guideline for how His people were to reverence Him and how they were to relate to each other. As and when the Psalmist thought about his relationship to the Lord, underscored in his heart and mind was the personal need to meditate on God's Law day and night (Psalm 1). When Jesus ministered, He reminded the people and religious leaders that He had not come to destroy the Laws of God (Matthew 5:17). When Joshua was being commissioned by the Lord (Deuteronomy 32:23) to assume leadership of His people, Moses reminded Joshua about the centrality of God's Law for his personal life and the corporate life of the people (Joshua 1:7-9). The mandate for Leadership contained precise directives:

1. Be strong and very courageous.
2. Be careful to obey all the law my servant Moses gave you;
3. Do not turn from it to the right or to the left, that you may be successful wherever you go.
4. Keep this Book of the Law always on your lips;
5. Meditate on it day and night, so that you may be careful to do everything written in it. Then you will be prosperous and successful.
   Have I not commanded you?
6. Be strong and courageous.
7. Do not be afraid;
8. Do not be discouraged, for the Lord your God will be with you wherever you go.

Meditation on God and His Law were indispensable for knowing God and making Him known. If one decides not to meditate on God and His Law/Word, what alternative will one have to know God and His will/purpose? According to Charles Wesley: "We have no other argument, we need no other plea…" The psalmist prayed the correct response, Psalm 19:14, "Let the words of my mouth and the meditation of my heart be acceptable in your sight, O Lord, my rock and my redeemer."

Over the years, we all have met someone who meditates more on Soap Operas and Sports and can give detailed updates about either or both. If they are asked, in what way has God enriched your life today as you read His Word and meditated on it, most would either stare at you with a blank look or try to fabricate something that sounded Biblical or Spiritual.

Joshua, along with his lifelong friend Caleb, had patiently prepared for the day when entrance into and possessing of The Promised Land would take place. There is a secular philosophy of life that suggests: "The person who succeeds is not the one who holds back, fearing failure, nor the one who never fails, but rather the one who moves on in spite of his experience with past failures." Although Joshua and Caleb were champions of success after searching out Canaan, because of the people's rebellion, they had to wait in the wilderness until all of the rebellious adults had died. They would eventually have the privilege of leading the younger generation who had not rebelled to that place of promise and blessing.

There are hundreds and thousands of promises in the inspired Holy Scriptures. Some estimate the number of promises to be at least three thousand up to seventy-seven hundred. The actual count is not crucial. Paul summarized it best in Second Corinthians 1:20, "For no matter how many promises God has made, they are 'Yes' in Christ. And so through him the 'Amen' (so be it/Yes) is spoken by us to the glory of God." Another rendering of this text (AMP) is: "For as many as are the promises of God, in Christ they are [all answered] 'Yes.' So through Him we say our 'Amen' (our Yes) to the glory of God."

Joshua and Caleb knew they would encounter opposition in The Promised Land. They had seen the large warriors and the walled cities. They knew the obstacles they would encounter and have to conquer. The words they had reported to Moses and the people after returning from spying out the land with the 10 other spies was: "God helping us, we are well able to conquer it." That faith and confidence remained with them. Caleb expressed (Numbers 13:30): "Let us go up at once and occupy it, for we are well able to overcome it." In Numbers 14:9, Joshua and Caleb expressed: "Do not fear the people of the land, for they are bread for us. Their protection is removed from them, and the Lord is with us; do not fear them."

Are you oriented to fear rather than faith? Are you more oriented to the daily news than you are to the Good News? What receives your attention and commitment? Let it be God Alone and His Word treasured in your heart.

19. Compliance

In the professional world and business operation, there are compliance and ethical codes for how a person is to conduct himself and how a business is to be ethically reliable. There are guidelines that need to be adhered to and practices that are to be marked by integrity.

When considering the character of Joshua and Caleb, many descriptions and definitions could be given. One that is consistent with their following the Lord wholeheartedly is compliance – "the act of conforming, yielding; conformity." They were men of integrity and ethical values. They did not allow themselves to cut corners or to misrepresent core values. Their foundational principles were beyond reproach and they were consistent in their lifestyle choices. They were strong men – in character and commitment. In addition to their spiritual strengths, they also had physical strength for their extended journey in the wilderness with the rebellious adults who defied God's purpose and best will for them.

In Joshua 14:10-12, Caleb makes an appeal to Joshua in which he said: "As the Lord promised, He has kept me alive these forty-five years since He spoke this word to Moses, while Israel wandered in the wilderness. So here I am today, eighty-five years old, still as strong today as I was the day Moses sent me out. As my strength was then, so it is now for war, for going out, and for coming in. Now therefore give me this hill country that the Lord promised me on that day." Caleb implicitly and confidently knew what it meant to "Be strong in the Lord and the strength of His mighty power" (Ephesians 6:10).

Caleb's witness reminded me of an old Hymn that emphasized readiness. In 1890, David E. Dortch wrote the words that described the character of both Joshua and Caleb.

The Refrain expresses the spiritual mindset of these faithful men of God.

Ready to go, ready to stay,
Ready my place to fill;
Ready for service lowly or great,
Ready to do His will.

In different generations, the Lord has had men of courage and spiritual commitment who represented Him regardless of the obstacles or threats of men. Hebrews 11 is a partial listing of some of those who were in compliance with God's standards and would not compromise them in any way. The bottom line is that God must be first and foremost in a person's focus and life.

We don't have a full narrative of what it meant when Joshua and Caleb were said to have been following the Lord wholeheartedly. By definition it means: "fully or completely sincere; enthusiastic; total commitment." They would've known God's revelation about Himself when Moses brought the Ten Commandments into the presence of the people. For the ramification of what that meant, Colossians 3:1-17 establishes how one is to live a full and consecrated life by seeking the things that are from above.

There is a citation about Jehoshaphat and his attempt to organize the nation so equity and justice would prevail (Second Chronicles 19:4-7). He sought to return the people to the Lord. One of the principles he established with the judges was (Vs. 6-7), "Consider what you do, for you judge not for man but for the Lord. He is with you in giving judgment. Now then, let the fear of the Lord be upon you. Be careful what you do, for there is no injustice with the Lord our God, or partiality or taking bribes." He wants there to be integrity and equity among those who oversee justice among the people. This is an aspect of doing things God's way, taking Him seriously and always following Him wholeheartedly. As one observes the cultural fragmentation of our day, it would be a great encouragement if there were several who dotted the horizon of the world – men of principle and commitment – who would not be thwarted by the obstacles of mankind; who would not fear any foe. Men of courage, commitment, integrity, whose lives are being lived beyond reproach. Men who would labor on without fear, weakness or compromise. Are such men available today – men who will do The Master's will? Horatius Bonar (1843) wrote about such men whom the Lord was seeking so they would serve Him...

Go, labor on: spend, and be spent,
Thy joy to do the Father's will:
It is the way the Master went;
Should not the servant tread it still?

Go, labor on! 'tis not for naught
Thine earthly loss is heavenly gain;
Men heed thee, love thee, praise thee not;
The Master praises: what are men?

20. The Master's Plan

Joshua and Caleb always knew there would be a day when the last adult who was part of the rebellion would die and be buried. They knew this was God's judgment upon a fearful and recalcitrant generation. The rebels epitomized lack of discipline and having an obstinate and uncooperative attitude toward any authority. Their recalcitrance was not just directed at Moses, Aaron, Joshua and Caleb. They wanted nothing to do with the plan of God for them. This would not be unique just to them.

To a future recalcitrant generation, the weeping prophet Jeremiah would convey God's Word of assurance and appeal – Jeremiah 29:11-14. God's people were in captivity and controlled by the Babylonians. To them, the Prophet speaks the words of hope from the Lord: "I know the plans I have for you, declares the Lord, plans to prosper you and not to harm you, to give you a future and a hope. Then you will call upon Me and come and pray to Me, and I will listen to you. You will seek Me and find Me when you search for Me with all your heart. I will be found by you, declares the Lord, and I will restore you from captivity and gather you from all the nations and places to which I have banished you...I will restore you to the place from which I sent you into exile." Will they hear and heed the word of the Lord? Being affirmative will fulfil their hopes – being negative will continue their oppression and helplessness.

God was the same for the children of Israel who left Egypt and is the same for us today. He has plans for one's good and not evil so that there will always be an occasion for hope and a future result of blessing. The children of Israel rejected that entire premise and promise of the Lord. That was also true of other generations. It was brutally true in the life of Christ as

He came to His own and His own refused to receive Him (John 1:11-12).

In the mid-1800s, E.S. Elliot wrote a hymn about the birth of Jesus Christ and no rooms being available in Bethlehem for His birth. The refrain is significant and could be a prayer we offer from our hearts to the Lord in this day: "Oh come to my heart Lord Jesus, there is room in my heart for you."

The Lord wanted the children of Israel in the wilderness to make room in their hearts for Him. He wanted them to conform their lives to His plan for their future. Their children, for whom they thought they were exercising a better choice and plan, would one day enter The Promised Land and receive the inheritance their parents refused. If only their parents had shown regret and repentance before the Lord. If only they had changed their mindsets so they could make room for the Lord and His assurances. If only they had some measure of faith to move forward in His direction.

Joshua and Caleb had stated their faith when they told the people that the Lord had removed the Canaanite's strength and defense and the people of God could readily possess the land. In actuality, the Israelites had no faith and very little confidence in the Lord. As a result, the adult population gradually died and their children, one day soon, would follow Joshua and Caleb into The Promised Land.

There is a gospel song that that contains reference to the final Promised Land and one's safe arrival there. Some of the lyric is: "There is coming a day...What a day, glorious day that will be...What a day that will be, When my Jesus I shall see, And I look upon His face, The One who saved me by His grace; When He takes me by the hand, And leads me through The Promised Land, What a day, glorious day that will be."

The issue remains the same today – Do you receive Jesus Christ and His plan for your good so you will share in His future and hope for you? Will you act on The Master's Plan or on your own alternative to it? Will you surrender your recalcitrant attitude and be receptive of His grace, mercy and admission into The Promised Land of eternity?

In 1926, Earl B, Marlatt wrote the words to a Hymn that asks a question in the stanzas and gives the acceptable response in the refrain. How do you respond to The Master?

> Are ye able, said the Master,
> To be crucified with Me...?
> Are ye able, when the anguish
> Racks your mind and heart with pain...?
> Are ye able when the shadows
> Close around you...?

Refrain Response:

> Lord, we are able. Our spirits are Thine.
> Remold them, make us, like Thee, divine.
> Thy guiding radiance above us shall be
> A beacon to God, to love and loyalty.

21. First Steps

There is a well-known statement that indicates: "The journey of a thousand miles begins with the first step." Conversely, "This same truth is applicable for the short journey as well." Some practical counsel is given in terms of this truism. "If you wait for things to happen, probably, nothing will happen. You have to take the initiative and act. You need to take the first step, and then the other steps will follow." There are several courses of action that can be followed. All of them require personal and inner-motivation, willpower and a commitment to self-discipline. Solomon offered counsel about the required willpower and self-discipline (Proverbs 6:6-11).

> "Go to the ant, O sluggard; consider her ways, and be wise. Without having any chief, officer, or ruler, she prepares her bread in summer and gathers her food in harvest. How long will you lie there, O sluggard? When will you arise from your sleep? A little sleep, a little slumber, a little folding of the hands to rest, and poverty will come upon you like a robber, and want like an armed man."

The lack of inner-motivation, willpower, and self-discipline relegates one to be classified as a sluggard who will ultimately experience increasing poverty. There are questions the lazy person should consider, think about and pray over. Questions, such as: What do I visualize as goals I can reach and tasks I can accomplish? Do I need a job and am I actively seeking one? Have I made viable plans regarding the purchase of basic necessities of life and put them to good use for me and my loved ones? Am I willing to act upon the negative habits that I need to change? Talking about change rather than doing something about it is added folly by the sluggard.

In the narratives about Joshua and Caleb, there are no indicators of them giving any space for sluggard behavior. When one is committed to be faithful and is wholeheartedly walking in the ways of the Lord at all times and in all matters, there is no need for directions being offered by anyone, especially by those who have rebelled against the Living God and His faithful servants. During the forty-year journey in the wilderness, there are very few references to what either Joshua or Caleb said. They said it all when the 12 spies gave their reports. When the ten spies took opportunity to report negatives present in the land, they had forgotten that they went beyond their assignment. They were to be more like land surveyors rather than critics of the venture. Joshua and Caleb stated that which is basic to faith and confidence in the Lord. Despite the fact of the fortified cities and strong people, their report was God is able and He will make the way where the other ten spies see no way. Caleb stated it succinctly and well: "We are well-able to overcome it,"

The error and folly of the ten was that they had a grasshopper mentality. They failed to look at the greatness and vastness of God. They chose to look at the fortifications and those who defended the cities and concluded it was a wrong direction and venture. It's not a surprise that in their report to Moses and the people that they would say (Numbers 13:33). "We saw giants there. We seemed like grasshoppers in our own eyes, and we looked the same to them." Grasshopper mentality will always give rise to sluggard-type reactions and limited activity. It led them to conclude that their "first-steps" should be in the direction from whence they came (Egypt) rather than toward Canaan (The Promised Land) with the Lord leading, guiding and protecting. Will the Lord make a way where there seems to be no way for His people? Yes! It is His plan for their good, future and on-going hope.

21. First Steps

The principle of God enunciated in Isaiah 30:19-21 was as valid for the children of Israel in their journey toward Canaan as it was in the day of promised restoration as written and spoken by Isaiah to a rebellious people of his day. The prophet declared: "He will surely be gracious to you at the sound of your cry. As soon as he hears it, he answers you. And though the Lord gave you the bread of adversity and the water of affliction, yet your Teacher will not hide himself anymore, but your eyes shall see your Teacher. And your ears shall hear a word behind you, saying: This is the way, walk in it, when you turn to the right or when you turn to the left."

It is a truth and principle repeated by Jesus Christ in Matthew 7:13-14, "Enter by the narrow gate. For the gate is wide and the way is easy that leads to destruction, and those who enter by it are many. For the gate is narrow and the way is hard that leads to life, and those who find it are few." In a very real sense, the first-steps toward entrance into Canaan, the land promised to God's people who were captives in Egypt, was narrow in that none of those who rebelled and complained about the plan were permitted to enter the land they had resoundingly rejected. Their children would be admitted – led by Joshua and Caleb – into the land of their future and hope. Their first step would move them to a great faith and confidence in God. Their fear of the unknown would be transformed to faith – if God says it, we will do it. This first step would also lead them onto many additional steps and further miles in their journey to possess the land and to gain their inheritance. Faith is the victory that overcomes – not just for the children of Israel – but also for you and me today. The Hymn writer expressed it well...

Each step I take my Savior goes before me,
And with His loving hand He leads the way...

At times I feel my faith begin to waver,

James Perry

When up ahead I see a chasm wide.
It's then I turn and look up to my Savior,
I am strong when He is by my side…

He holds the key that opens up the way,
That will lead me to the promised land.

Refrain:

Each step I take I know that He will guide me;
To higher ground He ever leads me on.
Until some-day the last step will be taken.
Each step I take just leads me closer home.

22. New Horizons

As mentioned earlier, we have no indication of the activities done by Joshua and Caleb with the younger generation. It would've been a good period of time to disciple these children about the ways and plans of God for them. It could've been a time to rehearse the advantages of possessing the land and the things seen during its exploration. Younger generations can be very receptive to the experiences of the past and the lessons learned from them. A guideline and requirement for older men is given in Titus 2:2, "Older men are to be sober-minded, dignified, self-controlled, sound in faith, in love, and in steadfastness." In other words, they are to be examples for the next generation to whom the torch of faith is to be passed. In Titus 2:6-8, Paul reminds Titus to "urge the younger men to be self-controlled." The special word for Titus was, "Show yourself in all respects to be a model of good works, and in your teaching show integrity, dignity, and sound speech that cannot be condemned."

Hopefully, this was part of the faithful ministry being done by Joshua and Caleb with the younger generation. They were preparing them for the new experiences they would encounter and for all the new challenges as they entered Canaan.

If Joshua and Caleb were discipling the younger generation, it would be reflective of the Laws of God and their application for His people. The Book of Deuteronomy would serve as their primer as they came to understand more about God and how he wanted His people to interact with one another. While the people were aware of what was taking place at the time of the Exodus due to the plagues and the required blood on the doorposts of their dwellings, they were a long way from spiritual maturity. They did have the amplification and applications of the Law given in the Book of

Deuteronomy. Compliance with the Law was necessary if they hoped to benefit from the promises, provision and protection of God available to them.

The Biblical Christian today has an advantage of gaining a greater definition of the spiritually mature life because of the ministry of Jesus Christ and the inspired writings of Scripture. The writer of Hebrews (6:1) urged his recipients: "Let us go on to maturity." There is a further guideline in Hebrews 10:23, "Let us hold fast the confession of our hope without wavering, for he who promised is faithful." This was missed by the first generation in the Exodus and care had to be given so that the next generation would move forward in faith rather than fear, and with hope rather than doubt.

Two epistles of Paul are very helpful in developing the theme of spiritual maturity - Philippians and Colossians. In Philippians 1:9-11, Paul wrote to the believers: "And this is my prayer: that (1) your love may abound more and more in knowledge and depth of insight, so that (2) you may be able to discern what is best and may be pure and blameless until the day of Christ, filled with the fruit of righteousness that comes through Jesus Christ to the glory and praise of God." Absolutely necessary and a firm foundation upon which ones life should be built. The Hymn writer, John Rippon (1787), addressed the foundation upon which one's faith and hope rests when he wrote:

> How firm a foundation, ye saints of the Lord,
> Is laid for your faith in His excellent Word!
> What more can He say than to you He hath said,
> You, who unto Jesus for refuge have fled?
>
> Fear not, I am with thee, O be not dismayed,
> For I am thy God and will still give thee aid;
> I'll strengthen and help thee, and cause thee to stand
> Upheld by My righteous, omnipotent hand.

To have a focus on a new horizon geographically is alright, but it is much more vital for one to have a focus on a new horizon in terms of one's relationship to Jesus Christ. When Paul wrote about spiritual maturity to the Philippian believers, he emphasized that spiritual maturity is always and only achieved by becoming more and more like Jesus Christ, The Westminster Shorter Catechism No. 35 asks, "What is sanctification?", the response given is: "Sanctification is the work of God's free grace, whereby we are renewed in the whole man after the image of God, and are enabled more and more to die unto sin, and to live unto righteousness." It is an ongoing process for the remainder of one's earthly life.

Paul made mention of one gaining the full knowledge of Jesus Christ (Philippians 3:12-14). He allows himself to be transparent, maybe even vulnerable, when he indicates that he has not obtained all of what he is writing about but he forgets about past victories and growth as he strains forward toward what is ahead. To attain it, he remains focused and fixed on the goal so he can win the prize for which God had called him in Jesus Christ.

In Colossians 2:6-10, Paul emphasizes the need to continue living one's life in Jesus Christ. It entails being rooted and built up in Him. As this is occurring, one will be strengthened in the faith and will be noted as one who overflows with thanksgiving. Paul summarizes: "For in Christ all the fullness of the Deity lives in bodily form, and in Christ you have been brought to fullness."

It was this type of knowledge (concept) that the younger generation in the wilderness needed to learn about God; being enabled to live and walk by faith, and becoming saturated with all of the promises of God. This spiritual maturing process will serve them well as they cross over into Canaan and as they become established as a nation. How will they receive these truths? Will they be ingrafted into their thinking and belief system? When they face barriers, obstacles and challenges, how will they react and respond? Will they be inclined to say: "We can't!" Or will their faith journey prepare them to respond: "Our God is able and He will make a way for us?"

In a devotional about the dangers of comparisons, Charles Swindoll wrote (July 16, 2019), "We do not dare to classify or compare ourselves with some who commend themselves. When they measure themselves by themselves and compare themselves with themselves, they are not wise." His text of reference was Second Corinthians 10:12 (NIV). He went on to observe, "God, our wise and creative Maker, has been pleased to make everyone different and no one perfect. The sooner we appreciate and accept that fact, the deeper we will appreciate and accept one another, just as our Designer planned us."

This was part of the discipleship lesson the younger generation needed to hear and apply. The new horizon would very soon become their new reality. They would have to be unified in focus and goal as they possessed the land gifted to them by the Lord. Will it be their reality? If they keep on looking to the Lord and His plan, they will be successful. They will learn this lesson from the example of Joshua and Caleb who had all their lives followed the Lord wholeheartedly.

23. A Journey Ends

Transitions are never easy especially when it pertains to one's life work. Those who have been deeply involved in a journey and are a member of a particular generation will naturally like to experience the fruition of those labors. I suspect this was partially in the mind of Paul when he wrote about the response to the Gospel for which he had labored. Above all else, he wanted to see unity among the believers. An issue had arisen causing diversity and disunity. People were emphasizing who had the greatest spiritual influence in their lives. Paul addresses spiritual maturity (or their lack of it) in First Corinthians 3:4-7, "For when one says: I follow Paul, and another, I follow Apollos, are you not being merely human? What then is Apollos? What is Paul? Servants through whom you believed, as the Lord assigned to each. I planted, Apollos watered, but God gave the growth. So neither he who plants nor he who waters is anything, but only God who gives the growth."

As the years passed and the rebellious generation has been dying, the new horizon of the Promised Land looms larger and larger. Many people may have assumed that Moses, since he had led the Israelites throughout their Exodus and wilderness wanderings, would be the one who would get them to the God-appointed destination. That wasn't to be and a major transition would take place. Moses made this transition known in Deuteronomy 31:1-3, "Moses continued to speak to all Israel. And he said to them: I am 120 years old today. I am no longer able to go out and come in. The Lord has said to me: You shall not go over this Jordan. The Lord your God himself will go over before you. He will destroy these nations before you, so that you shall dispossess them, and Joshua will go over as your head, as the Lord has spoken."

To all of the people, Moses went on to share an admonition and a word of encouragement: "Be strong and courageous. Do not fear or be in dread of them, for it is the Lord your God who goes with you. He will not leave you or forsake you." Will they heed his words? Will they be accepting of the leadership of Joshua as they enter Canaan? Will the influences of their rebellious parents be manifested in this younger generation? Will the Lord be their focus and will He receive allegiance, loyalty, honor and glory from them? Will this be an instance where it can be said: "You can take a person out of the wilderness but you cannot take the wilderness out of the person?"

As Moses surrenders the reigns of leadership to Joshua, the remaining question is how much of generation one been passed on to generation two. Have the lessons in the wilderness been learned? Has the Law of God been inculcated into the hearts, minds and lives of the children who at age forty-plus would enjoy their new lives in The Promised Land? Have the parents told their children of their great mistake in rebelling against God's plan and His leaders? Did they share any regret that they let their fears short-circuit their faith? Would the new generation be more committed to the Lord and His ways than their parents?

The Lord had Moses share a very grim picture of the future. Deuteronomy 31:16-18 contains the Lord's concern about the potential behavior of the generation entering The Promised Land. "The Lord said to Moses: Behold, you are about to lie down with your fathers. Then this people will rise and whore after the foreign gods among them in the land that they are entering, and they will forsake me and break my covenant that I have made with them. Then my anger will be kindled against them in that day, and I will forsake them and hide my face from them, and they will be devoured. And many evils and troubles will come upon them, so that they will say in that day, Have not these evils come upon us because our

God is not among us? And I will surely hide my face in that day because of all the evil that they have done, because they have turned to other gods." The Lord is indicating that temptations within the new horizon culture will have an influence on many of the people and those influences will infiltrate their belief system and be in contradiction to the first four commandments of God (the focus on relationship with God alone and required Sabbath observance). They have a choice of daring to be different and live as the Lord's people or willingly adapt their lives and lifestyle to the culture that exists. They chose to adapt to the culture rather than establish God's Law and plans as the infallible rule for faith and practice. As a Post Script to all he has shared, Moses adds (Deuteronomy 31:27-29), "Behold, even today while I am yet alive with you, you have been rebellious against the Lord. How much more after my death! Assemble to me all the elders of your tribes and your officers, that I may speak these words in their ears and call heaven and earth to witness against them. For I know that after my death you will surely act corruptly and turn aside from the way that I have commanded you. And in the days to come evil will befall you, because you will do what is evil in the sight of the Lord, provoking him to anger through the work of your hands."

At the direction of the Lord, Moses wrote a song for the people to sing. It would be a reminder of God's expectation for them. After the song was written and sung, Moses then shared in Deuteronomy 32:45-47, "When Moses had finished speaking all these words to all Israel, he said to them: Take to heart all the words by which I am warning you today, that you may command them to your children, that they may be careful to do all the words of this law. For it is no empty word for you, but your very life, and by this word you shall live long in the land that you are going over the Jordan to possess."

These words should not only be rehearsed to that generation but to all succeeding generations throughout history. The force of what Moses concludes is:

(1) Command these things to your children;
(2) Teach and tell them to be careful to do all the words of the Law;
(3) These are not empty words for you;
(4) They are your very life;
(5) By these words you will live long in the land you will possess as well as in the presence of God from this point onward.

I somewhat suspect that Joshua and Caleb would be saying, Amen! The question is: How many of those who will possess the land agree and say: "So be it Lord!"? May we have the good sense to be in agreement with the Lord, His word and His plan. If we do, there will be unlimited and immeasurable blessing that we will realize as we live before the Lord and walk in obedience to Him.

24. Unfolding Plan

God is very gracious. Even though Moses was told by the Lord that he would not lead the people to possess the land, the Lord wanted Moses to know that his arduous journey had not been in vain. Moses was taken up onto a Mountain and permitted to see, gaze upon, enjoy and appreciate the land the Lord was giving to His people. Momentarily Moses' life will end. The details leading up to his death are recorded in Deuteronomy 34:1-6, "Moses went up from the plains of Moab to Mount Nebo, to the top of Pisgah, which is opposite Jericho. And the Lord showed him all the land, Gilead as far as Dan, all Naphtali, the land of Ephraim and Manasseh, all the land of Judah as far as the western sea, the Negeb, and the Plain, that is, the Valley of Jericho the city of palm trees, as far as Zoar. And the Lord said to him: This is the land of which I swore to Abraham, to Isaac, and to Jacob, 'I will give it to your offspring.' I have let you see it with your eyes, but you shall not go over there. So Moses the servant of the Lord died there in the land of Moab, according to the word of the Lord, and He buried him in the valley in the land of Moab opposite Beth-peor; but no one knows the place of his burial to this day." This was the final moment in the life of Moses. Even though he was not permitted to enter The Promised Land of Canaan, upon his death he was immediately ushered into the eternal Promised Land.

Joshua would now have the responsibility of leading God's people into the land. The statement of the Lord to Joshua is terse, Joshua 1:1-3 (ESV), "The Lord said to Joshua, Moses' assistant, Moses My servant is dead. Arise, go over this Jordan, you and all the people, into the land that I am giving to them, to the people of Israel. Every place that the sole of your foot will tread upon I have given to you, just as I promised to Moses." The Lord then issues a mandate as He commissions Joshua to lead His people. Joshua 1:5-7, "Just as I was with Moses, so I will be with you. I will not leave you or forsake you. Be strong and courageous, for you shall cause this people to inherit the land that I swore to their fathers to give them. Only be strong and very courageous, being careful to do according to all the law that Moses my servant commanded you. Do not turn from it to the right hand or to the left, that you may have good success wherever you go."

Success is one of those nebulous possibilities. The idea is for the entire effort to be a great success. Joshua knows it will be a success for him and Caleb. How will the people respond to the obstacles and challenges that are before them? There will be a tremendous number of people who will have to cross the Jordan River. There is no bridge across. There are no boats to charter. This will be the first opportunity for the people to exercise their faith and confidence that the Lord will make a way for them. Joshua is more comfortable in the role of a commanding officer for his militia army. But his role is now different. He is God's replacement for Moses. In Joshua 1:10-11, we find Joshua asserting himself as he "commanded the officers of the people to pass through the midst of the camp and issue them his command: Prepare your provisions, for within three days you are to pass over this Jordan to go in to take possession of the land that the Lord your God is giving you to possess." In three days they will embark to take possession of the land. Joshua sent out two spies to ascertain what is taking place in Canaan with special attention being given to Jericho.

The day arrived when Joshua lined up the people to cross the Jordan River. The directions are clearly stated in Joshua 3:2-6, "As soon as you see the ark of the covenant of the Lord your God being carried by the Levitical priests, then you shall set out from your place and follow it. Yet there shall be a distance between you and it…Do not come near it, in order that you may know the way you shall go, for you have not passed this way before. The distance mandated was 2,000 Cubits (a Cubit equals 18 inches; 2,000 Cubits was equal to 3,000 feet). Then Joshua said to the people, Consecrate yourselves, for tomorrow the Lord will do wonders among you. And Joshua said to the priests, Take up the ark of the covenant and pass on before the people. So they took up the ark of the covenant and went before the people."

The phrase, "you have not passed this way before" is significant for all generations in terms of knowing God's will and plan for one's life. The children of Israel are being urged on and commanded as to what they are to do and why they are to respond affirmatively. If we pause to look at our own lives, we would do well to remember the words of Psalm 18:30 "As for God, His way is perfect; the Lord's Word is flawless; He shields all those who take refuge in Him." Because of who God is, we should always be prompt to defer to Him and His Word. Why? Because His way is always perfect and His word is always flawless.

The Israelites were also directed to prepare for the journey. Have enough provisions for three days. The words that seem to attach to one another is: "Prepare to Possess." As these directions and commands are made known, the people are affirmative in their response: "All that you have commanded us we will do, and wherever you will send us we will go." The first chapter of Joshua closes with important and dynamic words: "Only be strong and courageous." In the last church where I was privileged to be Pastor, we had a Youth Pastor who did exemplary work with a group of children (some of whom were previously unchurched). We also had a Music Coordinator and Instrumentalists who added greatly to the ministry, especially the Sunday Evening activities. The young people had a favorite worship chorus and they would sing it with enthusiasm and with emphasis on the word "CRUSH." The lyrics included:

James Perry

Mighty warrior Dressed for battle
Holy Lord of all is He.
Commander in chief Bring us to attention
Lead us into battle To CRUSH the enemy.

Satan has no authority Here in this place
He has no authority here
For this habitation Was fashioned for
The Lord's presence - No authority here.

As it was with Joshua and God's people, my ongoing hope
and prayer is that these words are the reality and testimony of
these young people in their lives today. May the Lord grant it
for them and us!

25. Spies Sent Out

Before the Levites take the first steps into the Jordan River, Joshua sends out two men to see what is happening in Jericho. It is a risky but necessary mission. Jericho is a great walled city; fortified; and guarded by sentries. The men sent would have to be risk-takers and men of courage. Joshua 2:1 records their assignment: "Joshua secretly sent two spies: Go, look over the land, especially Jericho." The first thing these two men do is to stop in a house on the wall: "They went and entered the house of a prostitute named Rahab and stayed there." Why they chose her house as their immediate destination we are not told. The spies may have viewed it as a place where the least suspicion would be raised regarding who they were and why they had come to Jericho. The spies may have concluded that it was a place where they could gain knowledge of the city and the latest street talk that was circulating. For the spies, it served temporarily as a type of "safe-house" for them.

However, when strangers enter a city or facility it raises curiosity and suspicion. In Joshua 2:2-3, the king is told that two men from Israel have entered the city and Rahab's dwelling. The king surmises and concludes they have come to spy out the land. Rahab was asked if she had seen them and where they had gone. She fabricates a story that they had come but left the city and shortly thereafter the city gates were closed for the night. She urged the King and his men to chase after the two men quickly. Maybe they would be able to catch up to them. Meanwhile, she had hidden the spies under flax on her roof. When she deemed it was safe, she made ropes available so they could scale down the city wall and be safely on their way.

Rahab sought a covenant with the spies because of the information and help she had given them. Rahab gave them a word of encouragement and assurance (Vs.8): "I know that the Lord has given you this land and that a great fear of you has fallen on us, so that all who live in this country are melting in fear because of you." She then asks the men to swear an oath to her (Vs. 12-13) that she and her family would be remembered and spared when the Israelites entered Jericho to subdue the enemy and to possess the city. They respond (Vs. 14): "Our lives for your lives! The men assured her. If you don't tell what we are doing, we will treat you kindly and faithfully when the Lord gives us the land." They state a condition for her. The rope by which she lowered them was scarlet in color. The spies indicated (vs. 17-18) that she must put a scarlet cord in the window and all of her family members must be inside her house as well.

Rahab the harlot is mentioned in Matthew 1:5 as the mother of Boaz; Hebrews 11:31, for her having welcomed the spies in peace; and James 2:25, for her assisting them so they could escape. Most people would keep a person like Rahab at arm's length or a greater distance. Why? Because of the way she chose to earn income (as a harlot). When we do so, we need to consider the statement of Paul in First Corinthians 6:9-10, "Do not be deceived: Neither the sexually immoral nor idolaters nor adulterers nor men who have sex with men nor thieves nor the greedy nor drunkards nor slanderers nor swindlers will inherit the kingdom of God." Verses 9-10 taken out of context would allow that these types of people should be avoided and condemned because of the choices they made for their lives. However, Paul quickly adds in verse 11, "AND THAT IS WHAT SOME OF YOU WERE. But you were washed, you were sanctified, you were justified in the name of the Lord Jesus Christ and by the Spirit of our God."

The plan, way, will and grace of God are far different than those of His created beings. Paul reminds us in First

Corinthians 13:12 (NLT) "Now we see things imperfectly, like puzzling reflections in a mirror, but then we will see everything with perfect clarity. All that I know now is partial and incomplete, but then I will know everything completely, just as God now knows me completely." We need to be mindful of these Biblical principles as we minister in the name of Jesus Christ.

There is a tremendous contrast evident in what transpired in Jericho. There is provincialism regarding how the city was run and how the people were governed. The king was obviously concerned for the safety of the people and the needed protection for the city. He was also concerned for his own well-being even though he felt secure in his walled and fortified city. The king had to be aware of the children of Israel amassed on the other side of the Jordan River. The conclusion could easily be reached that sooner or later the children of Israel may cross the river and the city could be overrun. The other part of this incident is the work of providence. The ways and means of the Lord may not be fully known by the people but His schedule will be fulfilled in His time. Rahab's willingness to be of assistance was part of His plan both in the immediate and the long-term.

It would serve us well to remember that God is always in control of all He has created. God has a perfect plan and perfect timing for that plan to unfold and be executed. We should remind ourselves of some great truths regarding God's ability to do all His holy will. Psalm 147:5, "Great is our Lord, and abundant in power; his understanding is beyond measure." Jeremiah 32:17, "Ah, Lord God! It is you who have made the heavens and the earth by your great power and by your outstretched arm! Nothing is too hard for you." Daniel 4:35, Nebuchadnezzar reached a point where he confessed, "All the inhabitants of the earth are accounted as nothing, But He does according to His will in the host of heaven and among the inhabitants of earth; and no one can ward off His hand or say to Him: What have You done?" Ephesians 1:11 (NLT), "Because we are united with Christ, we have received an inheritance from God, for He chose us in advance, and He makes everything work out according to His plan." This is our confidence and hope in Jesus Christ.

26. A Covenant Promise

A covenant is an agreement between two or more people; a promise that is to be kept. When the spies were sent to Jericho by Joshua, they found a place of relative safety in the home of Rahab the Harlot. She probably knew instinctively that these two men were the advance men to see what awaited all of the children of Israel as they crossed the Jordan River. Rahab had protected and hidden these two men, even lied on their behalf, and lowered them over the wall so they could safely return to Joshua on the other side of the Jordan. Before they left her house, Rahab proposed the terms of a covenant. She asked that she and her family will be spared when Israel comes to Jericho. She lowered them down the city wall with a scarlet cord. The spies told her to place a portion of that scarlet cord in the window of her home and all in her home would be spared (Joshua 2:18-21). After they departed, she immediately attached the scarlet cord in her window.

When I first entered college and began my journey of preparation for ministry, my Bible teacher was very dynamic as he stressed in class and his syllabus The Scarlet Cord Of Redemption throughout Scripture. In recent years, Jews For Jesus (October 1, 2001) posted a portion of that concept focusing on The Scarlet Cord. The author of that Newsletter, Carter Corbrey, wrote: "A slim scarlet cord dangling in a window might not trigger thoughts of deliverance. That is, unless you were Rahab, a Gentile woman living in a home built into the wall of the ancient city of Jericho over three thousand years ago. Rahab's scarlet cord was a sign to the approaching Hebrew armies to spare her family because she did not put her faith in walls, but in the God of Israel…"

That scarlet cord represented redemption for a handful of Gentiles…Following are just a small portion of Scriptures that foretold Jesus, who came to hang on Calvary, even as that scarlet cord hung from the window. Through Him alone, Jews and Gentiles can find redemption from sin.

The first messianic promise, that the "seed of woman" (not a natural mode of conception) will bruise the head of the serpent, is found in Genesis 3:15; further elaboration on the miraculous birth of this future deliverer is seen in Isaiah 7:14; the fulfillment found in Jesus is written in Matthew 1:18-21.

The Passover Lamb described in Exodus 12:1-28 points to Christ as our Passover (1 Corinthians 5:7) and also provides a ceremony upon which our Communion is based (Luke 22:7-20).

The Day of Atonement, with the scapegoat and the ram described in Leviticus 16, pictures a messianic promise further elaborated upon in Psalm 103:12 and fulfilled by Jesus as described in Romans 5:11.

Rahab's scarlet cord (Joshua 2:17,18; 6:17, 22-23) is a foretaste of how redemption will also come to faithful Gentiles. Rahab's faith was rewarded with the astounding honor of being placed in the genealogy of Jesus (Matthew 1:5), she is honored yet again by mention in the Hebrews 11.

The Suffering Servant of Isaiah 52:13-53:12, also detailed in Psalm 22, foretells the suffering of the Messiah Jesus described in Luke 23.

Jonah's experience in the great fish (Jonah 1:17) is seen as a "type" for the coming Resurrection. Prophecy also points to the resurrected Messiah (Psalm 16:10). The link between Jonah and Jesus is revealed in Matthew 12:40.

The slain shepherd described in Zechariah 13:7 foretells what will happen to the Messiah, the "shepherd." Jesus claims to be that shepherd in Matthew 26:31. Revelation 7:17 shows the Lamb and the Shepherd as One.

At the moment when the two spies were with Rahab, there was no way the long-range deliverance and redemption could've been understood by the spies. The covenant made with Rahab demonstrated that no one is beyond the amazing grace of God. As the old rescue mission preachers were wont to say: "God is able to save from the gutter-most to the uttermost." These were and are true words that are part of The Scarlet Cord of Redemption.

Ligonier Ministries shared the following in one of its studies on covenants. "The covenant of redemption is the agreement made between the members of the Trinity in order to bring us salvation. Under this covenant, the Father plans redemption and sends the Son in order to save His people. The Son agrees to be sent and to do the work necessary to save the elect (John 10:17–18), and the Spirit agrees to apply the work of Christ to us by sealing us unto salvation (Eph. 1:13–14). The covenant of redemption is one of the greatest examples of God's grace that we have. The Father, Son, and Spirit did not have to pledge to each other that they would bring to us salvation. But when they did, they guaranteed that it would happen. Remember that the grace of God was working on our behalf long before we were born."

In this regard, Paul expressed it clearly and succinctly in Ephesians 2:1-10 (NLT), "Once you were dead because of your disobedience and your many sins. You used to live in sin, just like the rest of the world, obeying the devil, the commander of the powers in the unseen world. He is the spirit at work in the hearts of those who refuse to obey God. All of us used to live that way, following the passionate desires and inclinations of our sinful nature. By our very nature we were subject to God's anger, just like everyone else. But God is so rich in mercy, and he loved us so much, that even though we were dead because of our sins, he gave us life when he raised Christ from the dead. (It is only by God's grace that you have been saved!)…"

The words about The Scarlet Cord of Redemption have been meaningfully written in a Hymn by Fanny Crosby.

James Perry

Redeemed, how I love to proclaim it!
Redeemed by the blood of the Lamb;
Redeemed through His infinite mercy,
His child and forever I am.

Henry W. Baker wrote similarly about The Scarlet Cord of
Redemption.

Redeemed, restored, forgiven,
Through Jesus' precious blood,
Heirs of His home in heaven,
Oh, praise our pardoning God!

Figuratively, may you prominently display The Scarlet
Cord of Redemption in the window of your soul. This is one
way others will see and know that you belong to Jesus Christ.
It will exhibit that you have been delivered by Him and are
living your life for Him.

27. Stepping Out

After approximately 40 years of wandering in the wilderness, the moment to move into The Promised Land was now at hand. There was an important protocol to be followed. The Ark of the Covenant represented God being in the midst of His people. In Exodus 25:10, Moses received the command to build an ark of acacia wood. The tablets of the law were to be placed within this ark. On the top of the ark, was a golden plate. Two cherubim, with raised wings and facing each other, covered the ark. From the place between the two cherubim God promised to speak to Moses. This place on the lid was also referred to as the Mercy Seat. Once a year a priest would enter the holy of holies and sprinkle blood from a sacrificed animal on the Mercy Seat to atone for the sins of Israel.

The Ark of the Covenant was designated to lead the children of Israel into The Promised Land. Joshua directed that the Ark must be 3,000 feet in front of the people (Joshua 3:4) leading the way as God leads His people to His land of promise. The specific reason given (Joshua 3:5) was so "You will know which way to go, since you have never been this way before." Joshua informs the people: "The ark of the covenant of the Lord of all the earth will go into the Jordan ahead of you...And as soon as the priests who carry the ark of the Lord, the Lord of all the earth, set foot in the Jordan, its waters flowing downstream will be cut off and stand up in a heap."

This will represent steps of faith. The generation that died in the wilderness had difficulty believing that the Lord would divide the Red Sea so they could cross it safely. They were more certain that the pursuing Egyptian Army would have them trapped against the sea and kill them (Exodus 14:10-14). Moses made a significant statement as the people expressed their anxiety and fear. He said: (Verses 13-14), "Fear not, stand firm, and see the salvation of the Lord, which He will work for you today. For the Egyptians whom you see today, you shall never see again. The Lord will fight for you, and you have only to be silent." The significant phrase by Moses is: "stand firm, and see the salvation of the Lord." The Lord is ready to deliver you from your slavery. Redemption is just a faith-step away. Moses reassured the people that because the Lord was fighting on their behalf: "The Egyptians whom you see today, you shall never see again. Just be silent and trust the Lord to fight for you."

Steps of faith are necessary in one's life if goals are to be achieved and destinations reached. Joshua and Caleb were absolutely certain of that reality. These two men, along with others whom they had influenced, never doubted that they would reach The Promised Land and settle in their inheritance. It was almost forty-five years of walking by faith for both Joshua and Caleb before they reached their goal. They rested their hope on the promise given by the Lord to Moses. Their confidence was renewed many times over as they saw the hand of the Lord intervene in miracles performed through Moses and situations resolved by those who loyally followed the Lord through the wilderness.

On the other side of the Jordan was Rahab and those crammed into her home on the wall. Their hope and confidence was in the scarlet cord she was directed to hang in her window. The scarlet cord would secure deliverance for her and her household. Similarly, the Ark of the Covenant carried by the priests would secure the deliverance of those who followed it across the river bed. That which represented God present in their midst would accomplish their safety and deliverance as they journeyed behind it by faith. The refrain of an old Hymn states the obvious: "Each step I take I know that He will guide me; To higher ground He ever leads me on.

27. Stepping Out

Until some-day the last step will be taken. Each step I take just leads me closer home." Those who achieve exploits for the Lord do so as they walk by faith and confidence in the Living God. It is living one's life within the framework of Hebrews 11:6, "And without faith it is impossible to please God, because anyone who approaches Him must believe that He exists and that He rewards those who earnestly seek Him." On so many occasions, Jesus raised the question with His followers: "Why do you have so little faith (Matthew 6:30, 8:26, 14:31, 16:8, 17:20)?" During a storm at Sea (Mark 4:40), Jesus confronted His disciples with two questions: (1) "Why are you so afraid?" and (2) "Do you still have no faith?" The issue was plain. Are the wind and waves, those things seen by one's sight, of greater significance than the power of God, that is only known and experienced by faith? A. W. Tozer stated: "True faith rests upon the character of God and asks no further proof than the moral perfections of the One who cannot lie."

An unknown source indicated from his point of view that: "Faith in faith is like a blind man walking across an unfinished bridge in the dark that doesn't reach the other side." Doing this would not only be dangerous but foolish as well. Eliza E. Hewitt (1890), in the Hymn, My Faith Has Found A Resting Place, penned these words:

> My faith has found a resting place,
> Not in device or creed;
> I trust the ever living One…

Refrain
> I need no other argument,
> I need no other plea…

> Enough for me that Jesus saves,
> This ends my fear and doubt...

111

James Perry

My heart is leaning on the Word,
The living Word of God…

Stepping out in confidence is possible because of one's
living faith and hope in a living Deliverer – Jesus Christ.

28. New Environments

The children of Israel have reached a crucial juncture as their wanderings in the wilderness are ending and entering The Promised Land begins. When one steps out by faith, there is always a new hope, a new confidence, a new horizon ahead and a new environment to develop. Before they entered this new environment they may have had times to reflect on the fears of their parents as they faced the challenge of the Red Sea. Their parents had allowed themselves to forget or ignore the presence of God in their midst - the Shekinah Cloud (the glory of divine presence) that led them during the day and the Pillar of Fire that provided them with both illumination for navigating during the night and protection from predators and enemies. Joshua was very careful in his instruction about The Ark of the Covenant leading the people into the Promised Land. It not only contained God's Laws but also represented the presence of God before the people. They were to follow the Ark because they had never traversed this way before (Joshua 3:4).

The new adventure that would lead them into the new environment that was about to begin (Joshua 3:14-17). "The people set out from their tents to pass over the Jordan with the priests bearing the ark of the covenant before the people, and as soon as those bearing the ark had come as far as the Jordan, and the feet of the priests bearing the ark were dipped in the brink of the water (now the Jordan overflows all its banks throughout the time of harvest), the waters coming down from above stood and rose up in a heap very far away...And the people passed over opposite Jericho. Now the priests bearing the ark of the covenant of the Lord stood firmly on dry ground in the midst of the Jordan, and all Israel was passing over on dry ground until all the nation finished passing over the Jordan."

Crossing the Jordan River was no small task. There were a great number of people who had to make that journey. The children of Israel were numbered by Moses and Eleazar the priest in the plains of Moab by the Jordan and near Jericho (Numbers 26:1-4ff). This was done shortly before Joshua would lead the people across the Jordan River and into The Promised Land. The Jewish adult males numbered 601,730 (Numbers 26:51). If that number is doubled to include the women, the total would be 1,204,460 adults. There is no estimate of the number of children but a reasonable guesstimate would bring the overall total to more than two million people. Added to the above numbers are the Levites. The number Levites was calculated (Numbers 26:52-63) and totaled another 23,000. "They were not listed among the people of Israel, because there was no inheritance given to them among the people of Israel" (Verse 62).

Joshua 4:1-7 records: "When all the nation had finished passing over the Jordan, the Lord said to Joshua, Take twelve men from the people...and command them, saying: Take twelve stones from here out of the midst of the Jordan, from the very place where the priests' feet stood firmly, and bring them over with you and lay them down in the place where you lodge tonight." There is an important pedagogical principle for this command. It pertained to the children who have made this important journey across the Jordan River bed. People tend to forget events and the significance attached to them. Gathering the Memorial Stones and erecting them on the shoreline of The Promised Land had a twofold implication: (1) so this will be a sign among you, and (2) When your children ask in time to come: What do those stones mean to you? - then you shall tell them that the waters of the Jordan were cut off before the ark of the covenant of the Lord. When it passed over the

Jordan, the waters of the Jordan were cut off. So these stones shall be to the people of Israel a memorial forever."

The Lord did not want the next generation to forget that which was done as a miracle of God. It would be good to frequently return to those Memorial Stones and to be reminded of God's Plan and Purpose for them and how He made it happen by His power. In some ways, the Israelites hadn't seen anything yet. Ahead of them was the walled city of Jericho that they would have to conquer. Would they be equal to that task? Could they, with limited weapons of warfare, conquer a fortified city that was secure behind a very large wall? Will they remember the steps of faith they had taken to reach this point? Could they – would they – keep trusting God to go before them and make the impossible possible? There is an interesting observation about the people in Joshua 4:10-11. It is a commentary about faith versus fear. The text states: "The people passed over in haste. And when all the people had finished passing over, the ark of the Lord and the priests passed over before the people."

"The people passed over in haste" does not represent their eagerness to finally be in a new environment with new challenges. It conveys the idea that as they entered the river bed, they probably had an eye on the waters of the Jordan that were heaped up and held only by the hand of God. This is the issue of faith for all generations. Has our faith subdued and conquered our fears? It's similar to the account in Mark 4 about the disciples in their ship that was caught in a storm at sea. Jesus was with them but He was asleep in the stern of the boat. The frustration and fear of the disciples emerged as they yelled out to Jesus: "Master – the tempest is raging; The billows are tossing high. Don't you care that we are perishing?" Jesus responded to them: "Of course, I care and you know that I do. He spoke to the effect of the storm and said: Peace! Be still!" Jesus said to His disciples: "Why are you so afraid? Have you still no faith?"

It is important for every follower of the Lord to keep in mind the words recorded in Psalm46:10, "Be still and know that I am God..." Put aside your frustrations, anxieties, fears and doubts. I AM your God. I AM with you! I AM your protector and guide. I AM your good Shepherd. Meditate upon that truth and remember His words. Know the constancy and intimacy of His perfect peace (Isaiah 26:3) for you.

29. Eagerness

When one is walking by faith in The Lord, there could be, should be, an eagerness and expectation regarding where the Lord is leading and what awaits those who reach the assigned destination. In a devotional (July 2019), Charles Swindoll posted "The Case Against Vanilla." He referred to Caleb in particular and wrote: "Remember our old friend, Caleb? He was eighty-five and still growing when he gripped an uncertain future and put the torch to the bridges behind him. At a time when the ease and comfort of retirement seemed predictable, he fearlessly faced the invincible giants of the mountain (Joshua 14). There was no dust on him. Every new sunrise introduced another reminder that his body and rocking chair weren't made for each other. While his peers were yawning, Caleb was yearning." I love the last comment that when others his age were yawning he was still yearning to complete that which The Lord had for him to do. This is how it must be for those who faithfully follow The Lord wholeheartedly.

There are certain concepts that go hand in hand with each other. Examples include faithfully and wholeheartedly; eagerness and enthusiasm; patience and confidence; to know Christ and to make Him known; knowing God's will and conscientiously doing it. When Joshua and Caleb returned from spying out Canaan (Numbers 13:26-33), they did not gloss over the challenges and the effort that would be required to possess the land. Despite those obvious concerns, they were eager to go forward because God would intercede in their behalf. The strong and the mighty (the Canaanites) would not have sufficient will or strength to prevent God's people from inheriting their land. God going before them would cause the fortifications to be ineffective and to crumble before them.

Joshua and Caleb continued to urge the people to listen to them and proceed immediately. Their eagerness was based on the presence of God with them and His securing the victories on their behalf. The people rejected their urging and wanted to quit (Numbers 14). If anything, they wanted new leaders and a return to Egypt and the place they had known for most of their lives. This was their choice and expressed desire – stop where they were and return to the place from which they had fled.

There was an obvious void in their lives. There was no faith, no hope, no confidence in the Lord or His appointed leaders, no eagerness to gain their inheritance and the blessings associated with it. What did they choose to ignore? What did they need to know about eagerness? Why would they reject having enthusiasm to do or have something that was a gift from God to them? In being devoid of eagerness, they would also lack: enthusiasm, zeal, wholeheartedness, desire, earnestness, commitment, yearning, thirsting for, etc. With these being the character traits and DNA of the rebellious, they would also be unable, by extension, to embrace the words of Jesus in Matthew 5:6 (ESV), "Blessed are those who hunger and thirst for righteousness, for they shall be satisfied." (AMP) "Blessed (joyful, nourished by God's goodness] are those who hunger and thirst for righteousness (those who actively seek right standing with God), for they will be (completely) satisfied."

The Israelites lacked the eagerness to go on with the Lord and to trust His enablement. Had they done so, they would've accomplished exploits by His strength and power. The older generation would die and be buried in the wilderness. They came to an important threshold and refused to cross it. Their act would delay their children's entrance into The Promised Land by more than forty years. As they observed others dying, some may have had some regret. There could be no joy filling them and no peace in their mind because of the choice they had made. This lack of joy would be compounded when they objected to the food provided by the Lord for them. They wanted their Egyptian Gourmet choices from their past and not the Manna day after day.

Their experiences and actions in the wilderness journey can oftentimes be descriptive of the choices we prefer and the decisions we make today. In Galatians 5, the clear instruction is that the people of God are to walk and live by the enablement of the Spirit. In this spiritual journey, a distinction has to be made between the deeds of the flesh and the fruit of the Spirit. If one is eagerly walking by the enablement of the Spirit, the lusts and desires of the flesh will diminish and be removed as the fruit of the Spirit grows within one and brings one to complete fruition. It is similar to the words spoken by Jesus (John 15) that He is the vine and His people are the branches. The branches that are not showing the fruitfulness in that relationship are removed from the vine and cast aside. This is what occurred with the children of Israel in the wilderness. They chose barrenness over fruitfulness. It is what will occur with any one of us who makes a similar choice today.

Eagerness needs to be present in the lives of the Biblical Christian. In a passage on stewardship, Second Corinthians 8:11-12 (NLT), Paul urge God's people, "Let the eagerness you showed in the beginning be matched now by your giving...Whatever you give is acceptable if you give it eagerly." In terms of the Biblical Christian life, Paul urged (Ephesians 4:1-3 (ESV), "I...urge you to walk in a manner worthy of the calling to which you have been called...eager to maintain the unity of the Spirit in the bond of peace." A passage that should be a great motivator for the Biblical Christian today is Acts 17:11, "Now the Bereans were more noble-minded than the Thessalonians, for they received the message with great eagerness and examined the Scriptures every day to see if these teachings were true."

The point is that one should be seeking God's way rather than his own way. Mob rule, even if it is a majority as it was in the wilderness, should not be allowed to short circuit one's embrace of God's promise and power. When the Lord says "Go!" one must understand that He has promised never to leave or forsake one of His own. He will go with us as our Shepherd who is leading, guiding and protecting (See also: Isaiah 41:11-12). In the late 1800s, Mary Brown wrote the words of a hymn:

> It may not be on the mountain's height
> Or over the stormy sea,
> It may not be at the battle's front
> My Lord will have need of me;
> But if by a still, small voice He calls
> To paths I do not know,
> I'll answer, dear Lord, with my hand in Thine,
> I'll go where You want me to go.

At the very least, this is a goal and prayer each child of God should approach and embrace with eagerness. May He grant that each of us eagerly do His will and go where He wants us to go.

30. Overcoming Obstacles

Walking by faith and not by fear is not always easy. Faith will have to endure during the storms of life and the difficult situations that come one's way. When the unknown is encountered faith and fear can become entangled. I smile when I read Joshua 4:10 (NLT). The priests stepped into the Jordan River and the waters stopped flowing. A pathway of dry riverbed was available for the children of Israel to walk over to the other side. Two faith opportunities loomed before them. The water was heaped up to clear a pathway and the walled city of Jericho was within their sight. How would they cross to the other side? The text states: "The people hurried across the riverbed." Why hurry? Were they eager to get to Jericho? Or, were they fearful of the heaped up water suddenly cascading down upon them?

Once they are all safely on the other side, twelve men were designated to go back into the riverbed and gather twelve stones and bring them back to the shore. Why? The answer is Joshua 4:6-7, "This will be a sign among you. When your children ask you in time to come: What do these stones mean to you? Then you shall tell them that the waters of the Jordan were cut off before the Ark of the Covenant of the Lord...These stones shall be to the people a memorial forever." There were many things that God's people needed to remember and serve as a Memorial: The Sabbath Day to keep it holy; The Passover and the children recounting the significance of the blood sacrifice; and these Memorial Stones to remind the people of God's intervention on their behalf. Hopefully, the people in times to come will thoughtfully reflect and remember all of what God has done for them and requires of them as His people.

But now there is the walled city of Jericho blocking their path. How can they proceed on their journey with Jericho blocking their way? With limited resources for combat, how could they conquer the obstacle before them? First things first. Joshua 5:2-9 tells us that all the men of Israel had to be circumcised with a flint knife. Ouch! You can be certain there was some weeping and wailing as this was being done. Verse 8 indicates, "When the circumcising of the whole nation was finished, they remained in their places in the camp until they were healed." The healing process would take awhile. An adult circumcision could take up to three to four weeks to heal, sometimes longer if there is residual swelling. For an infant male child, it would take one week to ten days to heal. This was also a required sign of the Covenant Promise of God made to Abraham and his seed (Genesis 17). To glean the association of then with now, Galatians 3:29 states: "If you belong to Christ, then you are Abraham's seed and heirs according to the promise.

After the period of healing from the circumcisions and before they move toward Jericho, the Israelites must first observe The Passover (Joshua 5:10-11). Afterwards, Joshua, like Moses, will have a holy ground moment. Joshua 5:13-14 states that "When Joshua was near Jericho, he looked up and saw a man standing in front of him with a drawn sword in His hand. Joshua approached Him and asked: Are you for us or for our enemies? Neither, He replied. I have now come as commander of the Lord's army." Joshua knows implicitly that the time for conquering Jericho has come. How will the conquest be accomplished? What will be the most effective battle strategy?

Who needs a battle strategy when God is on one's side! God maps out the plan He wants fulfilled. Jericho had been locked down by the king. No one in and no one out. In Joshua 6:2-7, the Lord assured Joshua: "I have delivered Jericho and its king and its fighting men into your hands." God's plan was that the nation of Israel would march around the city walls – all the men of war leading the way and circling the city. This was to be done for six days. "Then on the seventh day, march around the city seven times, while the priests blow the trumpets. And when there is a long blast of the ram's horn and you hear its sound, have all the people give a mighty shout. Then the wall of the city will collapse, and the people will go up, each man straight ahead." Joshua informs the priests and the people what they are to do: "Take up the ark of the covenant and have seven priests carry seven trumpets in front of the ark of the Lord. And he told the people: Advance and march around the city, with the armed troops going ahead of the ark of the Lord."

The day of victory was coming closer. Verses 15-16 indicate what will take place and what the people are to do at a specific moment of time: "On the seventh day, they got up at dawn and marched around the city seven times in the same manner. That was the only day they circled the city seven times. After the seventh time around, the priests blew the trumpets, and Joshua commanded the people: Shout! For the Lord has given you the city!" Will this really happen? Is this really possible? Verse 20, "When the trumpets sounded, the people shouted. When they heard the blast of the trumpet, the people gave a great shout, and the wall collapsed. The people charged into the city, each man straight ahead, and captured the city."

But – wait a minute. There are two things that must be carefully observed. (1) Spare Rahab and all in her house because she helped the spies when they entered the land. And (2) Do not be tempted by the devoted things. No one was to take them for themselves or, if taken, everyone would suffer the consequences of God. Will everyone heed these words? Will someone be tempted by the gold, silver, brass and ornate trinkets/things of Jericho?

Joshua gave the direction to the two young spies who had been helped by Rahab to get her and all with her and bring them to a place of safety. The city of Jericho was set aflame and everything in it was destroyed. For them the Israelites, Rahab and her family, and all true followers of the Lord, faith is the victory that overcomes. This is why we must always walk by faith and never by sight.

31. Faith Faltering

It is so easy to get caught up in the euphoria of a great conquest and event. Whether it is sports, a performance, an accomplishment scholastically or in one's career, a moment of pride in accomplishment is understandable. When it occurs in matters of faith and carrying out the Lord's will for one's life, it is vital to remember that the source of the achievement and accomplishment is God. This is illustrated in the conquest of Jericho. Clearly Jericho's fall was choreographed by the Lord and done according to His specific directives. The parameters of what the children of Israel were supposed to do and the restrictions of what they should not do were clearly stated.

In a farewell address to the children of Israel, Numbers 43:20-23, Moses lists the members of the tribes who will take up arms and conquer the opposition after they cross the Jordan. They were to maintain this responsibility until the Lord had driven out the enemies before them and the land was subdued. Will it be an easy task? No! It will be an arduous effort. But once it is accomplished the land will become their possession. In verse 23, we learn there is a consequence for those who shirk from their actual duty while representing that they have fulfilled their obligation. Moses said: If you do not carry out your assignment, "Behold, you have sinned against the Lord, and be sure your sin will find you out." There are no secrets that one can keep from the Lord and no acceptable misrepresentations one can state before Him.

This is very important when it involves the faltering of one's faith. Something happened at Jericho that was contrary to the Lord's direction and Joshua's commands. For a brief while, no one knew about the faltering of faith. However, "your sin will find you out" is a haunting truth with which all must reckon. After the triumph over Jericho went smoothly, a cockiness emerged among some of the people. The next town to be conquered was Ai. Spies were sent to do reconnaissance and returned with the confidence that the entire army of Israel was not needed. Maybe two to three thousand would be sufficient to take care of that insignificant place (Joshua 7:3-5). Unfortunately, they forgot their consultation with the Lord and the result was an unnecessary and embarrassing defeat. The people of Ai chased the small army of Israel out of their town. They killed thirty-six men in the process. They were relentless in their pursuit and chased the small band of Israelites as far as they could.

Joshua 7:5-6 indicates the dismay that ensued among the people, Joshua and the elders. The "hearts of the people melted and became like water." To become disheartened implies that the people were depressed; hopeless; and losing their courage. Additionally, there was a deflation of their faith expectations as well. They thought they were invincible and could fight a battle with human strategy and conquer an inferior town. Joshua and the elders tore their clothes and fell on their faces before the ark of the Lord. If only they had gone to the Lord before the fact instead of after the defeat.

In my mind is a lingering question. Joshua and Caleb had always been strong advocates for doing things God's way. They wanted to be assured of His presence and His approval. Why did they not stand up and say: No? Why didn't they say: "We have not consulted with the Lord about Ai." We've trusted Him along this journey, let's not forsake doing so now. In the decision about Ai, the absence of any leader speaking up and saying "No!" is too illustrative of the culture and times of the twenty-first century. God is not consulted. Faith values are not considered! The arrogant attitude is that we will do things our way in the time of our choosing.

Joshua 7:1 reveals the reason the Ai defeat was predictable. It was not just a faltering faith by individuals. It was disobedience regarding the devoted things in Jericho.

31. Faith Faltering

"The people of Israel broke faith in regard to the devoted things, for Achan took some of the devoted things. And the anger of the Lord burned against the people of Israel." The haunting words of "be sure your sins will find you out" are now front and center before the people. Joshua 7:11-12 is God's indictment for what has been done. "Israel has sinned; they have transgressed my covenant that I commanded them; they have taken some of the devoted things; they have stolen and lied and put them among their own belongings. The people of Israel cannot stand before their enemies. They turn their backs before their enemies, because they have become devoted to destruction. I will be with you no more, unless you destroy the devoted things from among you." The words "they have become devoted to destruction" are powerful words by the Lord that required immediate attention. When faith is allowed to falter or become fractured, all kinds of negative consequences will ensue.

The people have to come before Joshua tribe by tribe until those who have taken the devoted things confess their sinful deed. In Joshua 7:20-21, Achan confesses his guilt: "When I saw the spoil (garment, silver. gold) I coveted them and took them."

Upon finding the devoted things, the guilty parties are brought to Joshua. The consequence for this disobedience and sin is harsh and immediate. Joshua 7:25-26 states, "Joshua said: Why did you bring trouble on us? The Lord brings trouble on you today. And all Israel stoned him with stones. They burned them with fire and stoned them with stones. And they raised over him a great heap of stones that remains to this day. Then the Lord turned from his burning anger."

Hebrews 10:29-31 serves as an insight into the mind of God as to why the grace of God should be desired and sought, whereas the faltering of faith should never occur. "How much worse punishment, do you think, will be deserved by the one who has trampled underfoot the Son of God, and has profaned the blood of the covenant by which he was sanctified, and has outraged the Spirit of grace? For we know him who said: Vengeance is mine; I will repay. And again: The Lord will judge his people. It is a fearful thing to fall into the hands of the living God." Achan had heard this truth, as had the children of Israel. Despite that, they risked taking matters into their own hands and allowed their faith to falter and become fractured in the process. Doing things God's way all of the time comes with a cost. Achan and all that was his was stoned and burned. Today, we may have to endure hardships until we return to the Lord, confess our sins and errors, seek His forgiveness and get on with always doing God's will for us and going in the ways that He has chosen for us. Our faith, trust and confidence in the Lord must be foundational and never compromised. Trust the Good Shepherd. He'll take great care of you.

32. Battle Strategy

It is always advantageous to know and follow God's plan. The city of Ai would face a day of accountability and retribution. Only this time, it would be God's way and not that of an arrogant, matter-of-fact group of younger men. Joshua 8:1-10 records God's strategy for the battle to take place in Ai. It began with the Lord telling Joshua not to be afraid or discouraged. It would be easy to have second thoughts following the recent debacle when two to three thousand children of Israel were routed by the army of Ai. God's strategy and plan was to go against Ai with the entire army. His words of assurance to Joshua are: "I have delivered into your hands the king of Ai, his people, his city and his land" (verse 1). The Lord also indicated that He would do to this smaller city precisely what had been done earlier to Jericho. There would be one exception. This time they have the Lord's permission to "carry off their plunder and livestock for yourselves."

The Lord's strategy for the battle was to essentially surround the town of Ai. A portion of Israel's Army was to locate themselves behind the city as an ambush force. Joshua was to take the major portion of the army and attack frontally. When the men of Ai come out against them, Joshua and his portion of the army would flee. This would entice the men of Ai to pursue them relentlessly. Their conclusion will be: "They are running away from us as they did before" (verse 6). At that point, the military force (approximately 5,000 men) behind the city would rise up from their ambush position and take the city. The Lord would then deliver Ai into their hands. After the city is taken, the army is to set it on fire. The assignment and task (verse 8) is unambiguous: "Do what the Lord has commanded you. See to it; you have my orders."

One of the lessons of faith is that one must be obedient to the Lord in all matters at all times. Disobedience is never acceptable if one is committed to walk in the ways of the Lord and to know his continuous blessings in faith, life and practice. Later, part of this lesson would be an emphasis of David as he wrote the words of Psalm 37:23-24 (NKJV), "The steps of a good man are ordered (established) by the Lord, and He delights in his way. Though he fall, he shall not be utterly cast down; for the Lord upholds him with His hand." Also, (AMP) "The steps of a good and righteous man are directed and established by the Lord, and He delights in his way and blesses him. When he falls, he will not be hurled down, because the Lord is the One who holds his hand and sustains him." These words represent the faith-walk in action for all people in all generations.

The king of Ai was alerted to the presence Joshua's army. He employed all the men of Ai and Bethel to come out against Joshua. The king of Ai was confident that they would triumph once again similarly to their previous victory. As they pursued Joshua (verses 18-19), "The Lord said to Joshua: Hold out your battle lance toward Ai, for into your hand I will deliver the city. So Joshua held out his battle lance toward Ai, and as soon as he did so, the men in ambush rose quickly from their position. They rushed forward, entered the city, captured it, and immediately set it on fire."

The men of Ai have a Gomer Pyle moment – "Surprise, Surprise." They looked back and saw the billows of smoke rising from their city. The ambush army of Israel that had set the blaze were now pursuing the men of Ai who found themselves in a pincer trap. Joshua 8:22 records: "The men of Ai were trapped between the Israelite forces on both sides. So Israel struck them down until no survivor or fugitive remained." The cost was great for Ai (verses 25-26), "A total of twelve thousand men and women fell that day, all the people of Ai. Joshua did not draw back the hand that held his battle lance until he had devoted to destruction all who lived in Ai." The king who had thought he had been spared, was hung on a tree. At sunset, his body was taken down, thrown outside the city gate and covered by a large pile of stones.

The battle strategy was a success. There was also a needed spiritual battle strategy. Today as then, it is important for there to be consistency in one's faith walk with the Lord. It will require the discipline for each new day so that one's spiritual eyes keep looking to Jesus, the Author and Completer of one's faith (Hebrews 12:2). It will require spiritual ears that are attuned to the Lord's voice and hearing: This is the way, walk in it, when you are thinking about turning to the right or to the left (Isaiah 30:21). It will also require that one is willing to meet the requirement of Scripture to seek, know and do God's will (Romans 12:2, Colossians 4:12). There must be the desire to grow in the grace and knowledge of the Lord Jesus Christ (Second Peter 3:18, Hebrews 6:1).

Don't you wish you could crawl into the heart, mind and will of Joshua and Caleb? Don't you wish you knew how they were nurtured so that the commitment of their lives was to faithfully and wholeheartedly follow the Lord? Don't you wish you knew precisely all that is necessary to be deemed as one who is wholeheartedly committed to the Lord? All of these questions and more remind me of a Stanza and Refrain of a Hymn that expresses:

> Jesus calls me – I must follow,
> follow every hour,
> Know the blessing of His presence,
> fullness of His power.

> Follow, I will follow Thee, my Lord,
> follow every passing day;
> My tomorrows are all known to Thee,
> Thou wilt lead me all the way.

Not only are these words a good reminder for one's personal commitment, they also serve to sharpen one's focus on how life is to be lived in the presence and by the power of God. We should remember that no task should be deemed as too small or too tedious. If our lives are fitting into God's plan for us, His power will always be present so we can accomplish all of what He wants us to be and do.

33. Staying Strong

Years ago, a popular cartoon was Popeye the sailor man. One of the songs Popeye sang often was: "I'm strong to the finish 'cause I eat my spinach, I'm Popeye the sailor man." Our children were never too encouraged by that song to eat much spinach but it helped just a wee little bit.

The changes in strength and the reality of aging are inescapable. Muscles become a bit flabby. Waistlines expand. Weight gain happens. Good posture begins to show some slouching. There is a saying: "Old age ain't made for sissies." The Medical Daily piles on with scientific processes that define biological aging: "Telomere shortening (a compound structure at the end of chromosomes); oxidative stress; glycation (the bonding of a sugar molecule to a protein lipid molecule); your body is succumbing to entropy (such as: degeneration; a measure of the efficiency of a system), And together they cause old age to be synonymous with old." Wow! Nothing much there to cheer the aging ones.

There are some exceptions to this process of aging. In Joshua 14 we learn that the land distribution west of the Jordan is reaching its conclusion. In verses 10-11, Caleb is speaking to his lifelong friend and reminds Joshua of the promise Moses had made to him about his designated portion of land. He couches his request in a very dynamic way when he said to Joshua: "Now behold, as the Lord promised, He has kept me alive these forty-five years since He spoke this word to Moses, while Israel wandered in the wilderness. So here I am today, eighty-five years old, still as strong today as I was the day Moses sent me out. As my strength was then, so it is now for war, for going out, and for coming in." With full awareness of the challenge that was awaiting him, Caleb assertively said to Joshua (verse 12): "Now therefore give me this hill country that the Lord promised me on that day, for you yourself heard then that the Anakim (large/giant-type people) were there, with great and fortified cities. Perhaps with the Lord's help I will drive them out, as the Lord has spoken."

What caused Joshua and Caleb to be noted as men who followed the Lord wholeheartedly? Joshua's task was to become the leader for the people as they entered the Promised Land. Caleb's task was to assist each tribe to get settled in their designated area and boundaries. These men were called to their special tasks by the Lord and they were fully committed to doing those tasks to the glory of the Lord.

After the tribes were settled, there was one more territory to be assigned. Caleb came to Joshua and made his appeal for his land. What motivated Caleb to make this statement? On what would he base his positive approach to his awaiting challenge? Caleb may have had some reflections about his forbears in Biblical History. God's patriarchs have always been great examples. Abraham was far more effective once he grew older. It was as he approached one hundred years of age that Sarah became pregnant with Isaac. Moses wasn't used with any measure of success until he turned age eighty. Afterwards, he would lead God's people for forty years during the Exodus and the wilderness journey. He did so with commitment and vigor.

Perhaps Caleb had learned in his faith-walk with the Lord principles of life that were serving him well and would see him through future tasks. One principle is a blessing he may have heard Moses state to Asher: "as your days, so shall your strength be." It may have been the principle that would later be shared by Solomon, Proverbs 19:10-11, "The fear of the Lord is the beginning of wisdom, and knowledge of the Holy One is understanding. For through wisdom your days will be multiplied, and years will be added to your life." Another basic principle that would later be shared by Paul (Philippians

4:11-13, ESV) was innately understood by Caleb, "I have learned in whatever situation I am to be content. I know how to be brought low, and I know how to abound. In any and every circumstance, I have learned the secret of facing plenty and hunger, abundance and need. I can do all things through him who strengthens me." He may have instinctively known James 4:14-15, "You do not know what tomorrow will bring. What is your life? For you are a mist that appears for a little time and then vanishes...you ought to say: If the Lord wills, we will live and do this or that." Caleb's faith-walk would also cause him to reach the conclusion: "Only one life will soon be past. Only what is done for the Lord will last."

Caleb approached Joshua remembering some of the basics in one's faith-walk: (1) The promise made by Moses in your presence; (2) Personal humility as he made the request; (3) His belief that the Lord would cause the walled city in his territory to crumble just as He had done at Jericho; (4) Confidence that the Lord would be his enabler to conquer any enemy and overcome any obstacle as he possessed (his inheritance) Hebron. Caleb's request to Joshua was (Joshua 14:12), "So now give me this hill country of which the Lord spoke on that day..." How will Joshua respond to Caleb's appeal? Will he honor the promise made by Moses? Will he believe his aging friend and faithful companion will have strength enough to possess that area? Caleb had emphasized his confidence and readiness. How will Joshua respond?

I can visualize that moment being one of emotion and gratitude. I can see Joshua embracing Caleb and sobbing together with him. They have done so much together and seen the hand of God working in their own lives and on the people's behalf. A distance will now part these two men of faith and wholehearted commitment. But then, there was the special moment when Joshua stepped back and blessed him, and he gave Hebron to Caleb...for his inheritance" (Joshua 14:13).

For us today, the Word of the Lord is the same as it was for Joshua and Caleb, Ephesian 6:10, "Be strong in the Lord and in the strength of his might (His mighty power)." There is a promised inheritance for those who are committed to the faith-walk with Jesus Christ. Peter added, (First Peter 1:3-4), "Praise be to the God and Father of our Lord Jesus Christ! In his great mercy he has given us new birth into a living hope through the resurrection of Jesus Christ from the dead, and into an inheritance that can never perish, spoil or fade. This inheritance is kept in heaven for you…"

34. Definitive Choice

Our lives are filled with many choices and decisions that have to be made each day. Some of these choices are based upon one's personal persuasion and selected context for life. For the one who has committed to being a Biblical Christian, the choices and decisions should be reached on the basis of Biblical principles and specifics enunciated by Jesus Christ. A good guideline is Psalm 119:1-3, "Blessed are those whose way is blameless, who walk in the law of the Lord! Blessed are those who keep his testimonies, who seek him with their whole heart, who also do no wrong, but walk in his ways!" Psalm 119:10-11, "I seek you with all my heart; do not let me stray from your commands. I have hidden your word in my heart that I might not sin against you." Psalm 119:105, "Your word is a lamp for my feet, a light on my path."

When Joshua is nearing the end of his earthly task, he challenged the people with the definitive choice they must make. We learn in Joshua 24 that he began by sharing with them a brief summary and history from the Lord. He reminded them of the Lord's intervention and provision for them as they possessed the land of promise. In Joshua 24:13-14, he reminded them of how they conquered the land: "I, the Lord, sent the hornet ahead of you, which drove them out before you—also the two Amorite kings. You did not do it with your own sword and bow. So I gave you a land on which you did not toil and cities you did not build; and you live in them and eat from vineyards and olive groves that you did not plant."

In verses 14-15, Joshua sets before them the logical choice that needs to be considered and made: "Now fear the Lord and serve him with all faithfulness...But if serving the Lord seems undesirable to you, then choose for yourselves this day whom you will serve, whether the gods your ancestors served beyond the Euphrates, or the gods of the Amorites, in whose land you are living. But as for me and my household, we will serve the Lord." The choice placed before the people was clear-cut and plain. I appreciate the NLT wording in verse 14: So fear the Lord and serve him wholeheartedly." To me, it is similar to the clear-cut and plain words written in First John 5:11-12, "And this is the testimony, that God gave us eternal life, and this life is in His Son. Whoever has the Son has life; whoever does not have the Son of God does not have life."

How will the people respond to the challenge of Joshua? How seriously will they take a serious God? Will they be able to maintain a spiritual commitment even when Joshua is no longer with them? The definitive choice that they are being challenged to make is not to the man Joshua but to the Living God Jehovah. If you were in the presence of Joshua and heard his farewell address, how would you respond? Would you be willing to get rid of the "stuff" that is repulsive to the Lord God?

The people responded to Joshua and said (verses 16-18): "Far be it from us that we should forsake the Lord to serve other gods, for it is the Lord our God who brought us and our fathers up from the land of Egypt, out of the house of slavery...the Lord drove out before us all the peoples, the Amorites who lived in the land. Therefore we also will serve the Lord, for he is our God." How will Joshua respond to the people? Will he encourage them and say, "Praise the Lord" for their statement? Surprisingly, Joshua sounds negative and a bit discouraging in Verses 19-20, "Joshua said to the people: You are not able to serve the Lord, for he is a holy God. He is a jealous God; he will not forgive your transgressions or your sins. If you forsake the Lord and serve foreign gods, then he will turn and do you harm and consume you, after having done you good." The people underscore their commitment by saying (Verse 24), "The Lord our God we will serve, and His voice we will obey."

34. Definitive Choice

Choices and decisions made before and to God are important. It is making a commitment and taking a strong stand. It seems as though the people interrupted Joshua and said to him (verse 21): "No, but we will serve the Lord." That's an emphatic statement and commitment. Is that an emphatic commitment you have made to the Lord? Joshua is quick to remind the people of what, in actuality, their professed choice means. If they had in fact chosen to serve the Lord, then they would comply with (verse 23): "Put away the foreign gods that are among you, and incline your heart to the Lord, the God of Israel." Joshua is making a very vital point about lip service versus existing habits and lifestyle. No one is capable of "serving the Lord" while making space in their lives for idols from their past traditions and practices. A definitive choice has to be made.

In verse 25-27, Joshua indicates to the people that the Lord has indicated to him that: (1) a covenant is being made with them; (2) the words of The Covenant are to be written in the Book of the Law of God; and (3) a large memorial stone under is to be set up under the Terebinth that was by the sanctuary of the Lord. Why? Joshua said to all the people: "Behold, this stone shall be a witness against us, for it has heard all the words of the Lord that he spoke to us. Therefore it shall be a witness against you, lest you deal falsely with your God." In effect, it will serve as both a memorial stone concerning God's Words and a stone of accountability based upon the words of the people. Joshua then sent the people away to the places of their inheritance. His farewell to them stressed that God will not share His glory with another (Isaiah 42:8 and 48:11) and all idols are to be removed from the homes and lives of the people in the Promised Land.

Having fulfilled his task assigned to him by the Lord, Joshua has completed that which he was given to do and said the words the Lord wanted him to say. Verses 29-30 records: "After these things Joshua the son of Nun, the servant of the Lord, died, being 110 years old. And they buried him in his own inheritance." An appropriate commentary and epitaph (verse 31) is: "Israel served the Lord all the days of Joshua, and all the days of the elders who outlived Joshua and had known all the work that the Lord did for Israel."

What will be the commentary and epitaph of your life and mine? What will generations that follow be caused to remember about us and our faith-walk with the Lord? At the very least, I hope mine will be that I followed the Lord wholeheartedly. How about you? What will yours be?

Epilogue

The Book of Joshua closes with the statement that Joshua died at the age of 110. At that moment, those who have been faithful to the Lord and followed Him wholeheartedly are few in number. One can imagine how helpful it could've been if Joshua had lived a few years longer and continued to lead and shepherd the people in their places of inheritance. In Acts 13:36 (NLT), a perspective on the death of a leader is given: "After David had done the will of God in his own generation, he died and was buried with his ancestors, and his body decayed." The key element given is "having done the will of God in his own generation." This applies to all followers of the Lord in all generations. Was Joshua indispensable to God's plan and will for His people? Yes! But after he had fulfilled his purpose and plan according to God's will for his generation, he died and was buried. Sad? Yes! However, God is executing His perfect plan in human lives and history. We should be willing for His will to be accomplished in each of us.

The people who would inherit The Promised Land had received an important instruction from the Lord spoken to them by Moses. The clear summation is in Deuteronomy 8:1-14 (NIV), "Be careful to follow every command I am giving you today, so that you may live and increase and may enter and possess the land the Lord promised...Remember how the Lord your God led you all the way in the wilderness these forty years, to humble and test you in order to know what was in your heart, whether or not you would keep His commands. He humbled you, causing you to hunger and then feeding you with manna...your clothes did not wear out and your feet did not swell during these forty years... Observe the commands of the Lord your God, walking in obedience to

Him and revering Him. For the Lord your God is bringing you into a good land—a land with brooks, streams, and deep springs gushing out into the valleys and hills; a land with wheat and barley, vines and fig trees, pomegranates, olive oil and honey; a land where bread will not be scarce and you will lack nothing; a land where the rocks are iron and you can dig copper out of the hills. When you have eaten and are satisfied, praise the Lord your God for the good land He has given you. Be careful that you do not forget the Lord your God, failing to observe His commands, His laws and His decrees that I am giving you this day. Otherwise, when you eat and are satisfied, when you build fine houses and settle down, and when your herds and flocks grow large and your silver and gold increase and all you have is multiplied, then your heart will become proud and you will forget the Lord your God, who brought you out of Egypt, out of the land of slavery."

Time passes very quickly and personal involvements can distract and cause one to lose one's focus on the Lord. Aging cannot be avoided. The leaders the Israelites had known and followed through the wilderness journey and those who led them into The Promised Land would no longer be with them. A recent devotional by Charles Swindoll shared the following thought: "Growing old is a fact we all must face." Physically, changes become more and more obvious. It is strange to feel and think inwardly from a younger perspective. It is difficult to recognize and admit that while the spirit may still be willing, the body is not cooperating. The devotional adds: "You prefer to sit more than stand; to watch more than to do; to forget your birthday rather than remember it! Mentally, the aging brain longs for relief. You can't remember like you used to, and you don't respond like you ought to. You start thinking more about yesterday and tomorrow and less about today." Sadly, this transfers over to one's allegiance to the Lord and obedience to His Word.

Epilogue

In one's relationship with the Lord, there will be some differences based on one's individual needs. The Lord has a perfect plan for each person. We are not robots. We are not carbon copies of some aging blueprint. John Wesley said that we each have an obligation to: "Do all the good you can, By all the means you can, In all the ways you can, In all the places you can, At all the times you can, To all the people you can, As long as ever you can." His words are inspiring and convicting. They are a worthy goal to think and pray about, as well as incorporating into our faith and life practice.

Being a follower of the Lord is not a spectator sport. We are not to be mere observers but rather doers for Him. We must stand for God's Word and principles rather than going along to get along. An example of taking a stand for God and His truth is in First Kings 18. Elijah is the principal character and Ahab is the king. The issue is the worship of Baal. There has been a prolonged drought throughout Israel because of this tolerated Baal worship. In the third year of the drought, Elijah appears and proposes a contest with the prophets of Baal. Elijah also appeals to the people (verse 21): "Elijah came near to all the people and said, "How long will you go limping between two different opinions? If the Lord is God, follow him; but if Baal, then follow him." And the people did not answer him a word." The NLT text paraphrase: "Elijah stood in front of them and said: How much longer will you waver, hobbling between two opinions? If the Lord is God, follow him! But if Baal is God, then follow him! But the people were completely silent." What a description – "completely silent."

What a vivid description of people who refuse to stand for anything but are too susceptible to fall for everything. The descriptive words are – "limping, wavering, hobbling" – indecisive. Additionally, they did not comment but remained completely silent. A comparison can easily be made about today's church. The consensus is just be all things to all people so the head-count will increase in the church. A sad result is that a generation will be cultivated that does not take a stand for anything and who will at some point begin to fall for everything that comes their way. The general preference is to sit as a spectator more than stand as a participant in and for a worthy cause. The choice made is to be content to watch more than being willing to do.

Charles Swindoll's Devotional concludes: "God decided to let you live this long for His purposes. Your aging is not a mistake made by Him nor is it an oversight or afterthought." In another devotional entitled Lifelines, he adds: "God, however, brings about birthdays not as deadlines but lifelines. He builds them into our calendar once every year to enable us to make an annual appraisal, not only of our length of life but our depth. Not simply to tell us we're growing older but to help us determine if we are also growing deeper. Wisdom comes privately from God as a by-product of right decisions, godly reactions, and the application of scriptural principles to daily events and circumstances. Wisdom comes, for example, not from seeking after a ministry but more from anticipating the fruit of a disciplined life. Not from trying to do great things for God but more from being faithful to the small, obscure tasks few people ever see."

This truth applies to most of us. The words of C. Austin Miles (1915) serve as a reminder and challenge:

Side by side we stand each day,
Saved are we, but lost are they;
They will come if we but dare
Speak a word backed up by prayer

Refrain:

So you bring the one next to you,
And I'll bring the one next to me;
In all kinds of weather, we'll all work together,
And see what can be done.
If you'll bring the one next to you,

Epilogue

And I bring the one next to me,
In no time at all we'll have them all,
So win them, win them, one by one.

Jesus Christ has made the choice and decision for us. It is His directive and commission that His people "go and make disciples." Nowhere did Jesus ever say: "Sit and watch. See what happens!" The decision made demands our attention, commitment and action. Take up your cross daily and follow Jesus.

About the Author

James Perry has served the Church with more than 54 years of continuous ministry. He attended Columbia Bible College (now Columbia International University) for three years; transferring to Covenant College, a new Presbyterian College in St. Louis, MO from which he graduated with a B.A. in Philosophy. After graduation, he enrolled in Covenant Theological Seminary where he received a B.D. in theology, and returned later for his M.A. He and his wife make their home in Centreville, AL; He has four children; 16 Grandchildren and 14 Great Grandchildren. He is the Author of 12 Books (all of which are available on Amazon).

www.ingramcontent.com/pod-product-compliance
Lightning Source LLC
Chambersburg PA
CBHW060832050426

42453CB00008B/657